HAROLD FALLDING is Professor of Sociology at the University of Waterloo, Ontario, Canada. A citizen of Canada, he was born in Australia and has also lived in the United States and England. He holds a B.Sc. in physiology and physical anthropology, a B.A. in English and history, and an M.A. in sociology, all from the University of Sydney; and a Ph.D. in sociology from the Australian National University.

Dr. Fallding has engaged in sociological teaching and research on four

Monographs of the Rutgers Center of Alcohol Studies

Under the editorship of MARK KELLER

This monograph series was begun as "Monographs of the Yale Center of Alcohol Studies" and Numbers 1, 2 and 3 in the series were published at Yale. Beginning with Number 4 the series has been continued as Monographs of the Rutgers Center of Alcohol Studies. The change conforms with the transfer of the Center from Yale to Rutgers University. The works published in this series report the results of original research in any of the scientific disciplines, whether performed at Rutgers or elsewhere.

No. 1. Alcohol and the Jews; a Cultural Study of Drinking and Sobriety. By CHARLES R. SNYDER.

No. 2. Revolving Door; a Study of the Chronic Police Case Inebriate. By DAVID J. PITTMAN and C. WAYNE GORDON.

No. 3. Alcohol in Italian Culture; Food and Wine in Relation to Sobriety among Italians and Italian Americans. By GIORGIO LOLLI, EMIDIO SERIANNI, GRACE M. GOLDER and PIERPAOLO LUZZATTO-FEGIZ.

No. 4. Drinking among Teen-Agers; a Sociological Interpretation of Alcohol Use by High-School Students. By GEORGE L. MADDOX and BEVODE C. McCALL.

No. 5. Drinking in French Culture. By ROLAND SADOUN, GIORGIO LOLLI and MILTON SILVERMAN.

No. 6. American Drinking Practices; a National Study of Drinking Behavior and Attitudes. By DON CAHALAN, IRA H. CISIN and HELEN M. CROSSLEY.

No. 7. Problem Drinking among American Men. By DON CAHALAN and ROBIN ROOM.

No. 8. Problem Drinkers Seeking Treatment. By EILEEN M. CORRIGAN.

No. 9. Drinking, Community and Civilization; the Account of a New Jersey Interview Study. By HAROLD FALLDING with the assistance of CAROL MILES.

No. 10. The African Beer Gardens of Bulawayo; Integrated Drinking in a Segregated Society. By HARRY F. WOLCOTT.

Drinking, Community and Civilization

Drinking, Community and Civilization

The Account of a New Jersey Interview Study

By
HAROLD FALLDING
with the assistance of
CAROL MILES

PUBLICATIONS DIVISION
RUTGERS CENTER OF ALCOHOL STUDIES
NEW BRUNSWICK   NEW JERSEY

3045

Library of Congress catalog card number: 73-620137
ISBN: 911290-41-9   ISSN: 0080-4983

Manufactured in the United States of America

Contents

List of Tables

Figure

Preface

IF THIS BOOK makes any lasting contribution to our understanding of drinking and abstinence it will flow from its sustained sociological viewpoint. I do not share the common belief that psychological factors in human affairs are somehow more ultimate, more determining or more accessible to manipulation than sociological ones. On the contrary, there is a real sense in which collective or corporate man has primacy. Individuals are not persons at all unless they give expression to superindividual meanings, to culture. While they may swim, so to speak, in this sea of culture and project a head or limb above it, they cannot move at all except by immersion in it. It is therefore supremely important to study the movement of the sea itself.

Notwithstanding a growing number of supporters for the science of sociology, its point of view is still very little understood or accepted. It says much, then, for people who assisted in this study, that they helped so willingly when they often could not be expected to understand whither it was tending. Acknowledgments are due to those citizens of the two study communities[1] who attended the public dinner where the research project was launched and who gave it endorsement. The representative of the Public Service Electric and Gas Company introduced the town to us in the first instance—he told us whom it would be most profitable to approach. Then there was a group of people who afterward were similarly helpful in making us both at home in the town and informed. Some of these also joined a larger set who supplied information when graduate students went to them with questions about the locality. Particularly generous in sparing time and attention were two employees of the weekly county newspaper, the pastor of the First Reformed Church, the Willowdale and Greentown Borough Clerks, four members of the Willowdale and Greentown Chambers of Commerce, a New Jersey Superior Court Judge, and the County Planning Director. Those persons who allowed us to interview them

---

[1] The two communities will be called Greentown and Willowdale. The use of pseudonyms was requested by some of the official facilitators of the study.

in their homes, either as pretest subjects or subjects of the study proper, must also be thanked.

During two summers, Rutgers graduate students assisted. These were Messrs. Joseph M. Conforti, Roger K. Craig, Edward Gelb, Thomas A. Kendall, Thomas D. Moore, Edward C. Mueller, Jr., and Misses Bonnie M. Davis, Nancy Golder, Florence J. Kellner and Dorothy Nakano. Mr. John S. Barovich, Jr., a student of Columbia University, volunteered assistance. The contributions of the interviewers, coders and people in the Rutgers University Sociology Laboratory must be acknowledged. Especially helpful in facilitating the technical procedures of analysis were Mrs. Zelda Cohen, Dr. Frank Fasick and Mrs. Coralie Farlee. Dr. Ian C. Ross wrote the computer programs that were used in the analysis. Toward the end of my labors on this study, when deadlines pressed, my 15-, 12- and 10-year-old daughters all undertook part of the mathematical computations involved in the statistical tests. The assistance given by Mrs. Frederica A. Coffey in the analysis of the data deserves special mention. Rarely would one find again her combination of willingness, resourcefulness, carefulness and cheerfulness. It was Miss Carol Miles who bore the main load of assistance through the whole course of the study, however. She directed her exceptional critical powers to all that was done, worked strenuously, and showed a stranger to America where to inquire and how to tread circumspectly.

A number of staff members of the Rutgers Center of Alcohol Studies facilitated work on the study; they cannot all be named. Dr. Selden D. Bacon, Director of the Center, Messrs. Raymond G. McCarthy, Mark Keller, Timothy Coffey and Robert W. Jones each helped wherever they could. Miss Adeline I. Tallau did not let the Center library lie fallow for me. Mrs. Margaret Wilson and Mrs. Dorothy Rottner took great care over typing the earlier drafts.

Certain faculty members in the Sociology Section at Rutgers were encouraging by virtue of the interest they showed, especially Professors Harry C. Bredemeier, Bernard Goldstein, Simon Marcson, Matilda White Riley, Earl Rubington[2] and Jackson Toby. Sociologists on other campuses were also very encouraging, Drs. Charles R. Snyder (University of Southern Illinois), Edwin M.

[2] Now at Northeastern University.

Lemart (University of California at Davis) and Milton A. Maxwell (now at the Rutgers Center of Alcohol Studies) in particular.

Support for the study was mainly supplied by the United States Public Health Service, Grant NIMH-5655; there was also a subsidiary grant from the Department of Health of the State of New Jersey. Liaison with the latter Department was facilitated by the willing efforts of Mr. William H. Harris, then Chief of the Alcoholism Control Program in the Division of Chronic Illness Control.

The complete draft of the manuscript was eventually prepared in 1971-72, while I was on sabbatical leave at the University of Cambridge. Financial support for this stage of the work came from the Canada Council. The excellent typing of the entire draft was the work of Mrs. Diane Pledger. A subsequent revision of that draft was prepared with great skill by Mrs. France Chouinard.

Finally, acknowledgment is given to the Editor for permission to reproduce in Chapter 1 much of an earlier paper, "The Source and Burden of Civilization Illustrated in the Use of Alcohol," QUARTERLY JOURNAL OF STUDIES ON ALCOHOL 25: 714-724, 1964.

HAROLD FALLDING

University of Waterloo
Ontario, Canada

Foreword

OVER the last 30 years a consistent picture of cultural patterns in drinking practices has been emerging. It has become increasingly clear that certain American ethnoreligious groups are able to drink alcohol with few socially dysfunctional consequences, whereas the predominant culture is not. The evidence for this conclusion and the reasons for it—how it works—require reexamination and updating at intervals. Professor Fallding has done considerably more than confirm others' results, however. He has undertaken no less a task than reconstructing a typology of the functions of taking alcohol. His emphasis is upon discerning to what extent alcohol serves positive, socially promotive functions. (What a delight to focus, for a change, on something positive!) The matrix of the "Dual Problem of Civilization" which he elaborates is quite consistent with notions of ego psychology and the growth potential for fulfillment of not only individuals, but whole communities. (In fact, one of the dimensions is borrowed part and parcel from Erik Erikson.)

Professor Fallding's conclusions contain many important implications for social change. They are precisely the issues which have stimulated the National Institute on Alcohol Abuse and Alcoholism at the Federal level to mount a national campaign for the prevention of alcoholism. We are calling the thrust of the campaign "Responsible Drinking," and concentrating upon such uses as, for example, Professor Fallding has classified under "Ornamental, Community-Symbolic Drinking." Perhaps we should be even bolder and actually advocate drinking alcoholic beverages for those who so desire. This study suggests, and we agree, that people *will* drink alcohol, and yet they are profoundly ambivalent about why they do so and what the consequences will be. I was particularly struck by one of the notions of abstinence. "I have suggested that community symbolic drinking is alternative to other ways of symbolizing solidarity, so there is presumably a type of abstinence which does not originate in opposition and which could be called indifference abstinence." To which we would add that there is no such indifference in imbibing!

The plea for greater community cohesion in order to deal with everybody's "Number One Drug Problem" strikes a welcome chord of response in us. One of the things we have learned very well during the first two years of operation of the National Institute on Alcohol Abuse and Alcoholism is the necessity for quality community organization efforts. In fact, for just some of the reasons outlined in this monograph, we have decided to require such a thrust in our treatment programs. This is not to slight the importance of diversity in American society; far from it. Rather, it is an effort to help people to live better in that community where they choose to be. There is a message for us here: it is that the "melting pot" needs to be recognized and utilized to build trust among neighbors to a degree which has never yet been attempted in the United States. This is practical, it can be done systematically, and its efforts can—and should—be properly evaluated in the broadest sense by anthropologists, sociologists, and virtually any other social-science discipline.

MORRIS E. CHAFETZ

National Institute on
Alcohol Abuse and Alcoholism,
Rockville, Maryland

Introduction

ALL too often purportedly social scientific studies of drinking, using elaborate quantitative techniques, yield only atomized and trivial information about the nature and significance of drinking practices in social life. The root problem, as I see it, is that these studies are typically undertaken by persons lacking the courage or capacity to conceptualize the larger social and cultural setting in which drinking takes place. Harold Fallding's research on drinking practices in two New Jersey boroughs, reported in this volume, stands in sharp contrast to such studies because it begins with a well-thought-out view of the source and burden of civilization, of the social structure and cultural values, and of the crucial historical developments affecting the communities investigated. The special virtue of his study is not to be found in the novelty of the research technique, which is quite typical in its reliance upon a sample survey, or even in the particular questions asked respondents about their drinking, many of which have been asked in other studies. It lies, rather, in his sensible and persuasive ordering of the seemingly discrete, isolated, and specific facts about drinking, gathered through field-work, into highly general patterns whose distribution, functions, and meanings can be effectively analyzed. And this, in turn, stems from an ability to relate drinking practices to a clearly articulated view of the total social and cultural structure.

Only in such a broad sociological perspective could Professor Fallding have evolved, systematically, the typologies of drinking and abstinence so fruitfully employed in this book. The typing of drinking as ornamental, facilitation, assuagement, and retaliation, though in some respects novel, has close affinities with an earlier classification developed by sociologist Robert F. Bales. But in creating a correlative typology which portrays distinct varieties of abstinence anchored in indifference, moral, religious, or respectability concerns, Professor Fallding has broken genuinely new ground in the sociological study of drinking behavior. As used in his research, these typologies enable us not only to see the distribution and significance of the different modes of drinking, as, for instance, in the dominance of facilitation drinking, but also to grasp the interplay between types of drinking and varieties of abstinence.

Another contribution of his research is Professor Fallding's careful investigation of the institutionalization of drinking and abstinence, which refers essentially to the social protection of practices by rewards and penalties. This aspect of drinking behavior is generally thought to be important by students of the subject and is repeatedly alluded to in the literature of alcohol studies. More often than not, however, the question of institutionalization is passed over without theoretical development or the addition of factual substance. The reader of this book will discover a great deal about the extent to which different types of drinking and abstinence are institutionalized in contemporary America. Suffice it to say here that when Professor Fallding goes on to make such broad inferences as problem drinking is "simply an outgrowth of the dependence on alcohol's assistance that is commonly endorsed," he has at least already provided solid evidence that, in the locales studied, types of drinking fostering such dependence are positively sanctioned and widely institutionalized.

Beyond a variety of lesser conclusions of substantial practical or theoretical import, the clear thrust of Professor Fallding's work is that the recovery of civilized meanings of drinking in America hinges upon the development of genuine community. In his own words: "The failures of civilization implicit in the institutionalization of facilitation and assuagement drinking are a failure fundamentally of community." Having glimpsed, through the study of traditional Jewish drinking patterns, something of the power of community to give civilized meaning to drinking, in Fallding's sense, and to constrain drinking pathologies, I am to a great extent persuaded by this conclusion and believe it to be consonant with the findings of a variety of other studies. However, inasmuch as Professor Fallding calls for a birth of community in America that transcends our society's complex social differentiation and fragmentation, he poses a significant and intriguing challenge to advocates of cultural pluralism. As Fallding himself observes, there has been far less waning of the forces of pluralism than experts of the last few decades anticipated. Now we are in a period marked by renewed interest among intellectuals in, and a variety of evidence of, the vitality of diverse ethnic, religious, and other communities, and a recognition of their importance in providing loci of social identity for millions of Americans. Yet, paradoxically, the very vitality of these diverse communities would appear, on a higher plane, to perpetuate the social fragmentation and barriers to relationships of trust that apparently underlie our society's dependence upon facilitation and assuagement drinking and the difficulty in creating and adopting more civilized drinking patterns. To those who value pluralism, as I do, perhaps the profoundest long-run question raised by Professor Fallding's study is how, in America, we can reconcile the apparent contradiction between the social reality and values of cultural pluralism, on the one hand, and the need, on the other hand, for a more embracing community to foster civilized meanings of drinking and constrain the pathologies of alcohol.

CHARLES R. SNYDER

Southern Illinois University
Carbondale, Illinois
July 1973

Chapter 1

Drinking and Civilization

IN what things men must be alike and in what things they can afford to differ, if they are to live fruitfully together, is far from being known. Since Durkheim wrote *The Division of Labour in Society* (8), many have glibly assumed that the mutual dependence arising from differences will substitute for the bond arising from likeness. Yet, I cannot believe this will ever be so—nor do I think Durkheim concluded his book believing it. The relation between the two sources of solidarity seems to be other than this. It is not rather the case that men welcome differences only among those they acknowledge to be of their kind, and that they do this because they expect to enhance their common wealth by a greater specialization? They may, thereby, tie themselves still more firmly together by an *added* bond—not an *alternative* bond. On the other hand, it is one of the acutest problems of human relationship to be tied by a dependence when no community exists.

A relationship lacking community to a marked degree may nevertheless have a modicum of fellowship and trust which is sufficient for its scope (as with the legal contract or the business deal). But where there is no fellowship at all, or fellowship insufficient for the scope of the relationship concerned, naked power obtrudes. Such power inhibits productive cooperation because of its capriciousness. Since the parties to the relationship strive with one another, they cannot know what to expect. It is impossible then for each one to make an expected contribution to a product. If they cannot go apart and yet find their association intolerable, they may be found delving for evidences that they are really "brothers under the skin." They will look for some affinity to affirm. Unless they find it, as they probably know, they will make themselves poor. *They cannot store up savings in the bank of civilization.*

1

The Source and Burden of Civilization

I have suggested elsewhere that civilization can be thought of as the dignifying of human existence through adornment (10, *pp. 106-108*). This is achieved by the exploitation of surplus to devise need-gratifications that are not strictly related to survival. Yet this possibility of civilization presents man with problems on two levels—I call them the *source* and *burden* of civilization.

The problem of source is to maintain a base of productive co-operation; that is, to maintain mutual trust in the face of numbers and specialization. To keep such a fount of trust open in the midst of the garden of civilization, men foster community among themselves. For community is not profitably regarded as a place. It is essentially a matter of people keeping their likeness in evidence, so that the solidarity from sympathy will counter the centrifugal forces of differentiation and scale. "The most elementary likeness is kinship and the rudimentary community is the kin group. When community has extended beyond this, it is because men were prepared to extend the kinship prerogatives to persons involved in one struggle with them. The struggle against the natural habitat and the struggles for the viability of race, class and faith seem to be the main ones which have served" (10, *pp. 106-107*).

By the *burden* of civilization I refer to the need people have to put their ornaments to an innocent use. It is possible for them to become enslaved by an inordinate or inappropriate use of these. "Man becomes dependent on things he has himself gratuitously made meaningful, and is degraded by his own trifles" (10, *p. 108*).

Alcohol is one of these products of surplus and the use to which it is put may be dignifying or not—and that not primarily because it can be intoxicating or addictive. Man does not need alcohol for survival in the way in which he needs oxygen or sleep. If we try to specify what it does for man and measure how functional or dysfunctional these effects are, our thinking could be misdirected if we assumed it to be a necessary accompaniment of his life. Horton (19) ascribed a function to primitive drinking because it was a source of relief from anxiety about subsistence or the threat in cultural contact. But this seems unsatisfactory for two reasons: first, because it treats drinking wholly in relation to a primary or survival need and, second, because it uses the term function simply to designate any effect and does not discriminate between positive function and dysfunction. It may be more rewarding to think of alcohol as only having a positive function in relation to some sort of elaborated secondary need.

Indeed, our whole scientific picture of man gains greatly in realism if we are prepared to remember that he enjoys a kind of two-tiered existence, with possibilities of fulfilment in detachment that are unknown on the relentless wheel of adaptive problem solving. In regard to alcohol, it might even be that its only functional use would be one in which (in one way of speaking) it had no function; that is, for people to drink as those who need not drink. Other uses than this it might have and has had; but insofar as they betoken an entanglement of man by his own ornaments, they would be counted dysfunctional. There is a whole class of practices that are ornamental in this kind of way, yet contain the possibility of excess or perversion, and a special interest attaches to their control through institutionalization. Drinking is one of them: loving, mourning, celebrating, playing, worshipping, rewarding and punishing, and theorizing—these are some others perhaps. Their study comprises a sociology of the golden mean or fine line, a sociology of civilization.

A Typology of Drinking

That the practice of consuming alcohol has been given different meanings has been recognized for some considerable time. But we still need a typology of uses. I suggest that the reports of drinking now available enable us to recognize four basic types, medicinal and other presumed technical uses apart. I am going to propose that only one of the four has possibilities of being socially functional, by virtue of the intention expressed in it. Whether its actual consummation is then made entirely functional depends on whether the people concerned have a sufficient understanding of alcohol to use it circumspectly. But three of the four uses of alcohol may be presumed dysfunctional categorically, because of the intention expressed in them. One of these, however (the one which becomes our second type) can find its defenders. The four types show alcohol being used to express four different outcomes of the dual problem of civilization. Figure 1 presents the four types graphically as they are located by the two axes of source and burden: trust–distrust and detachment–dependency.

The one benign type of drinking I call *ornamental, community-symbolic drinking*. In it trust and detachment are both sustained; the problems of source and burden are solved. In the second type, *facilitation drinking*, the problem of source is solved in that trust exists, but the burden of civilization is not mastered, in that the drinkers become dependent on their drinking. In both the remaining types, *assuagement drinking* and *retaliation drinking*, there is a more fundamental deficiency in that the problem of source is not met. Trust itself is absent and the drinkers use alcohol because of this fact; at the same time they become dependent on it.

There is no necessary wisdom in a social consensus, but what any group agrees to be of value it will protect. The protection of a practice by a set of rewards and penalties is what we understand by institutionalization. Societies have, then, an option as to whether they will try to institutionalize type 1 only or other types as well as or instead of it. The structural-functional question about drinking is

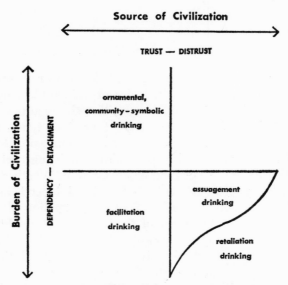

FIGURE 1.—*Alcohol Use Expressing Four Different Outcomes of the Dual Problem of Civilization*

to determine what proportion of a society's drinking is institutionalized and according to what patterns, what proportion is not, and
where each is located in the structure. It is as a contribution to
such a study of drinking that the present research is conceived.
I will try to characterize and illustrate the four types of drinking.

1. Ornamental, Community-Symbolic Drinking

Ornamental drinking symbolizes preexisting community. As such
we may take it to be symbolizing the most precious support men
can experience. It may be supernatural community or human community or both—and sometimes we see the celebration of both
closely associated. I would hardly think it appropriate, however, to
separate religious or sacred drinking from a more comprehensive
class which includes pure sociability drinking. For in either case
the drinking is ceremonial and symbolic: integrated with, subordin-
ate to and consequent upon the forging of solidarity. The alcohol is
not needed to generate any relationship but to express this preexisting solidarity generated by trust. Presumably, however, the
nature and effect of alcohol are what make it seem appropriate as
a symbol. Being fluid it is the same when divided, thus expressing
the drinkers' likeness with one another in the way that blood might
express kinship. It kindles and pleases, thereby expressing the confidence and delight they arouse in each other. And it represents the
abandonment which is possible within the fellowship of trust;
among those with whom one is free one may be this much more
free.

The symbolic role given to the alcohol suggests, however, that
it is strictly not necessary. Its use is disinterested and could be
made optional. The orthodox Jews' religious use of wine makes a
kind of prototype of this use: yet they may substitute unfermented
grape juice if wine is not available, and in various circumstances
other alcoholic or nonalcoholic beverages, or bread (2, p. 165). The
drinking may be whittled down to token proportions as in the
Christian communion. The common family meal, which presumably
is its ultimate model, may be made to suffice without it, as with the
Quakers and the Salvation Army. The drinking may remain em-
bedded in the meal, as with the Italians (21, 39). On the other
hand, among simpler peoples at any rate, the drinking may reach
intoxication quite regularly, as with the Camba (15), Chagga (37,

pp. 17-40), Papago (*37, pp. 172-184*) and Ainu (*37, pp. 187-220*).
This type of drinking seems to be not uncommon, in fact, among
primitives, for as long as contact leaves them relatively undisturb-
ed. As well as in the tribes mentioned, it has been described, without the intoxication, among the Azande (*37, pp. 3-16*) and Tiriki
(*30*).

Ornamental drinking still occurs on occasions at social gatherings
among ourselves, but its comparative rarity may be taken for a sign
of the eclipse of community among us.[1] One would hardly expect
it to be reinstated in advance of a restoration of real community.
We see what only amounts to a travesty of it in those who go to
their drinking, and impose the enjoyment of it on others, as if it were
a hanging. This is illustrated in the practice of trying to create community by setting up attractive bars instead of stirring people up
to faith and love. But nothing could be less sufficient for the genesis
of community than to supply the materials by which it could be
symbolized, if present.[2]

2. *Facilitation Drinking*

Facilitation drinking is to ease the person's integration into
society, with which he still identifies. It is essentially a matter of
helping to make difficult adjustments. Trust is present, but certain
individuals are unable to surmount internal barriers to participation
without a degree of alcoholic anesthesia. It is a type of drinking
about the sanctioning of which there can be ambivalence: one person can be of two minds over it and persons of tough and tender
conscience disagree. Presumably this is because a person cannot

---

[1] Bacon (1) has drawn attention to the special possibilities, as well as risks,
opened up for alcohol use by large-scale complex society.

[2] Bearing on the present question, although not, of course, identical with it,
is Field's (11) cross-cultural examination of the social characteristics of the
primitive tribes which observe relative sobriety. It is interesting that he found
them to be those exhibiting a number of indices of community solidarity, including the firm discipline of children. In my view, however, it is probably
not a distinction of the greatest significance whether primitive peoples drink
moderately or to intoxication. That may largely be a matter of their technical
control and understanding and their need for unrelieved order. What would
be of greater significance is the different intentions they might express by their
drinking.

finally take credit for his alcohol-aided courage (it is not in the last analysis *himself*) and also because such drinking is so uncertain in its outcome. For while the drinking may well break down reserve and coldness, or soften bereavement or humiliation, or make one feel a man, it does so only very temporarily and it can at the same time release hostile and other impulses which create trouble. The drinker has to leave himself wide open; to get what he wants from the drinking he must accept the risk of getting things he does not want besides. Made an habitual crutch, it is a vicious block to help and growth.

Where the drinking is defined in this way, mutuality in the drinking becomes important, and there is pressure on companions to drink in like manner. There may also be apprehension about people's induction into drinking and prohibitions against adolescent drinking. Presumably this is because seasoned drinkers do not want to see youthful innocence spoiled by a practice which they know to be morally dubious and dangerous.

There can be an open door and a possibility of two-way traffic between this type of drinking and the first type. Facilitation drinking may be conspicuously absent, however, when the first type is present. It seems to be absent among the Papago and Ainu, but present among the Camba, Azande and Chagga. It can be the main or only style of drinking in a society, as with the nomadic Mongols (37, *pp. 217-229*) or the Lunahuaneños of Peru (32). Many 19th-century Irish of the small-farm class are reported to have drunk mainly from this kind of impulse, the conviviality to which it sometimes admitted them being its consequence rather than its cause (2.) It may be significant that in these last three societies many families lived in social or physical distance from others.

3. Assuagement Drinking

Alcoholization is made the substitute for mutual trust and common purpose in assuagement drinking. Trust has become rare and many individuals are without social location. The unlocated person who is denied a sense of membership experiences demoralization and, with it, insatiability. It is as if persons who cannot *be* filling must *have* filling instead. They therefore abandon themselves to immediate gratification, to sheer excitement, in food, sex, possessions, distinctions, power, information, notoriety, mystical exaltations, drugs, alcohol intoxication.[3] The experiences are taken raw. They are stripped of the meanings with which they are customarily invested by institutional contexts and which make them a different thing. The filling is needed to block out the awareness that one is out of society: the compulsion for it stems, presumably, from the unrelievable emptiness. These various kinds of *glitter behavior*, as they might be called, make a category of reactions quite distinct from those represented in type 2 drinking (which is the case of inadequacy and the attempt to compensate for it) or type 4 (which, it will be shown, is the case of withdrawal from the game still in progress and retaliation against it, due to lack of reward).

Assuagement drinking is found where community is failing and the distinctive civilization fed by it is losing its appeal, due either to inner enervation or outer erosion. Primitive and peasant peoples in the culture-contact situation may drink this way: the Australian aborigines, the New Guinea natives, the Indians of Mexico (4), the natives of French West Africa (3). But members of the older and great civilizations can be affected in the same way. Some of the drinking in the later Roman Republic (23) and in modern France (27) perhaps give the typical instances. But much other European and American drinking now seems to have this character. Where else could we classify, for instance, the peculiar glazed encounter at some cocktail parties of strangers, rivals, enemies, deceivers? Bad faith, the supreme sacrilege in the eyes of those who drink to celebrate community symbolically, presents itself here very thinly veiled.

Assuagement drinking is a kind of false imitation of community-symbolic drinking. It is the direct pursuit of the communal or religious exhilaration without benefit of community or religion. It is rather like a compulsive re-creation of paradise by persons who feel excluded from it.

4. Retaliation Drinking

In retaliation drinking the person exploits the incapacitating power of alcohol in order to make himself a passenger on the sys-

---

[3] Excessive and compulsive eating, and the obesity consequent upon it, have been recognized as an alternative adjustment to addictive drinking (33, *pp. 9-11*). It is being suggested here that a whole range of pure-gratification pursuits might substitute for one another in insatiable individuals denied social membership.

tem. His drinking is the protest of distrust against the community which, though still viable, has failed to win the adherence of all its members by giving them the reward they consider their due.

This use of alcohol almost contradicts the facilitation use. While in that case the person invokes the aid of alcohol to set him in society, in this case he seeks to be set against it and make himself a charge upon it in retaliation. To this end he cultivates habitual intoxication to make himself a burden. The same revengeful impulse which might bring some to suicide leads in other cases to self-inflicted incapacitation which stops short of death, and habitual intoxication is presumably only one of the possible expressions of this (25, 28). Some isolated, individualistic inebriates come here. Skid Row drinkers also. These can make a wistful, paradoxical case in that, insofar as they create traces of community among themselves, the same drinking as effects their rejection of others symbolizes a flickering acceptance of one another.[4]

SOME IMPLICATIONS OF THE TYPOLOGY

In view of the divergent, even contradictory, possibilities in alcohol use, and considering the precariousness of civilization itself, it is not surprising that the production of alcohol has left man with a problem on his hands for which he has no simple or single solution. It is probably because, somewhat like an iceberg, drinking has three submerged negative possibilities for the one positive, that the prohibition and abstinence movements have won what following they have. They represent periodic reactions to abuse which see the risks of abuse as outweighing the possibilities of benefit. A temperance movement, in the true meaning of the word, would aim for restrained drinking rather than abstinence. Yet it may be destined to turn into an abstinence movement if the society concerned lacks the genuine community which could give the only rationale for ornamental drinking. McCarthy and Douglass (22) have shown how the modern temperance movement progressed from moral suasion purely against drunkenness caused by spirits to moral suasion against drinking any form of alcoholic beverage, and thence to political prohibition. Standing on its own, "moderation" has no concrete meaning and no legitimization; it can scarcely be a constrain-

---

[4] Rubington (29) has described the new, though fugitive enough, solidarity which Skid Row drinkers can create.

ing norm. Meaningful rather than moderate drinking may be what is needed if drinking is to remain decorous.

I represent these four types of drinking in terms of their cultural significance and avoid giving any independent consideration to the state of physical or psychological involvement of the drinkers. For instance, whether Jellinek's (20) medical condition of alcoholism is engendered by one type more than another would be a matter for empirical determination. (While sheer habituation to alcohol use in any of the types might conceivably expose a person to alcoholism, there does seem to be a suggestive affinity between the loss of control Jellinek ascribes to alcoholism and the insatiability of assuagement.) But it is my object to suggest that, whether they ever conduce to such personal pathology or not, the last three types of drinking are indices of social pathology because of the failures of civilization in which they are implicated. Social pathology is sui generis.

A TYPOLOGY OF ABSTINENCE

Making a typology of abstinence is not as easy as making a typology of drinking, especially since we do not have comparable studies of it. But one may think of certain types of abstinence by analogy with the types of drinking they reject. This can be at least partly justified by the fact that abstinence is often an avoidance practice. As such, it may take its nature from its image of something to be opposed. I have suggested that community-symbolic drinking is alternative to other ways of symbolizing solidarity, so there is presumably a type of abstinence which does not originate in opposition and which could be called indifference abstinence. This abstainer just does not find it necessary to celebrate community loyalties by drinking: perhaps he does not find it frugal or pleasant, perhaps it simply seems redundant. Although as an abstainer he does not drink, he might not be unwilling to: at any rate if he has any unwillingness it does not stem from objection to what he takes to be unavoidable abuse in drinking.

There may be, on the other hand, one large class of abstinence which focuses opposition on one or more of the three dysfunctional kinds of drinking and supposes either that all drinking is like that, or that most of it is, or that it is almost bound to turn into that. This might be called protesting abstinence, and it may subdivide according to which of the three forms of drinking the objection is focused on. If exception is mainly taken to drinking for facilitation, drinking may be viewed either as a character weakness or as involving an irresponsible forfeiture of self-control, and this might be called moral abstinence. If it is to assuagement drinking that exception is mainly taken, drinking may appear to be the enemy of spiritual answers to social demoralization; it may be regarded with horror as something diabolic. Let us call this religious abstinence. (But it will have to be remembered that religious abstinence is that which is thus defined: it is not necessarily the type of abstinence observed by a religious person.) If exception is mainly taken to retaliation drinking because it characterizes low-status "bums" and "drunks," we might call it respectability abstinence. Later I will be aiming to show how frequently the above types of drinking and abstinence were exemplified in a sample of cases.

Chapter 2

The Communities in a Locality

THE PEOPLING of the United States speaks eloquently of limits being set to tolerable association by the presence of like-mindedness. The founders came to the New World because their neighbors could not bear to associate with them and because, all too soon, it had proven mutual. Others who migrated subsequently came for similar reasons. Of course, there were many who came for the living space their crowded homelands denied them; yet these, after migration, were unsuspectingly faced with the same kind of question as the others. How could they live in the New World with so many characters unsympathetic to themselves?

THE PURSUIT OF COMMUNITY IN AMERICA

It is Handlin's (13, 14) thesis that the diverse locality allegiances that had afforded the immigrants community back home, yielded in the New World to a more pervasive and inclusive community of common language and culture. In a way that they had not experienced before, Apulians became Italians, Thracians Greeks, Poznaniskers Poles. Yet, this phase of the more-embracing ethnic community was only transitional. Men and women delved for an even more profound affinity. They found it eventually in the religions that had nourished some of their cultures separately. Irish, Poles and Italians were assimilated as Catholics; English, Germans and Scandinavians as Protestants; people of a variety of nationalities as Jews. To be *in community* in the United States meant to be one of these.

Herberg (16) pursues this dénouement to a still later final phase. He sees a delving beyond the faiths even to a core of spiritual values and moral ideals common to the three, which Americans might affirm together as the "American way of life." He warns that we should not mistake this kind of community affirmation for religious commitment, and this point is well taken. But it is not neces-

13

sary that we overlook the fact of the affirmation, and its occurrence is of immense sociological interest. It testifies to the pursuit of a communal unity in the United States which has been no less persistent or necessary to its life than the pursuit of the political union. Yet, while it might be expected to progress, the trend is probobly not as advanced as Herberg makes out; nor will that kind of consensus necessarily displace the faiths or serve in place of faith.

If visitors to the United States, from nations with a single or dominant faith, miss between Americans the ease and gentleness they expect in social intercourse, it is perhaps because of the persisting cultural plurality. Because they cannot assume that their profoundest convictions are shared, Americans are prone to anxiously hold them out of view—and this can make the exchanges between them superficial and staccato. When a smothered issue bursts into the open, this evasiveness can even trigger violence. Americans are very often made aware that what they share *as Americans* does not include a great deal of what they share with smaller sections of the people. Much of the blame for the difficulty of life in America that is directed at things like industrialization, urbanization, bureaucratization and rapid change would be most properly directed at this, in my opinion.

The splintering of a people into what I am calling *communities*, on the basis of likenesses shared, is roughly equivalent to what Weber (38, *pp. 424-429*) meant by "status groups." Shibutani (31) has called them "worlds." They represent a principle in social structure that has been too much neglected, especially in view of their importance in supplying the dynamic of politics. (Although, of course, they are often recognized in political studies as "interest groups.") In these groups Durkheim's principle of "mechanical solidarity" (8, *pp. 70-110*) materializes; yet without examining them very carefully, we are too prone to say that they are categories and not groups at all. But if, in a more inclusive group, one sector differs from another in any characteristic, the sectors can become competitors for influence in the group that binds them both. The men may oppose the women, the young men the old, the practical types the mental types, the town folk the country folk. Such distinguishing traits may be legion, but the politically important ones are those that mark out blocs of people who are potentially able to manage an economy of their own.

The grounds of community mentioned early in Chapter 1 are selected on this basis. Kin groups of clan dimensions, tribes or nations that exploit the resources of a territory together, races, classes and faiths, these can, at the one time, bind people together in supportive ingroups and make them highly competitive in their outgroup relations. For it seems that the obverse of community is war —a thing we nearly always forget when we praise the one and deplore the other. The ingroup begets the outgroup, and it can only break through that dilemma to the extent that the qualification for ingroup membership approaches universality.

Drinking and Abstinence in Relation to Communal Ties and Rivalries

Communities like the above played a conspicuous part, of course, in the history of American drinking. Gusfield (12) has shown what line-up in the electoral struggle finally secured the Eighteenth Amendment that imposed National Prohibition in 1919. Those who came to dominance in that action were Protestants, of the rural middle-class, and "old" in the sense of belonging to a kindred long-established in America. The Eastern upper classes, the Catholic and Jewish immigrants and the urbanized middle class were all over-ridden.

Gusfield is also of the opinion that this ascendency was short-lived (12, p. 8):

"The repeal of the Eighteenth Amendment gave the final push to the decline of old middle-class values in American culture. Since 1933, the temperance movement has seen itself fighting a losing battle against old enemies and new ones. In contemporary American society, even in his own local communities, it is the total abstainer who is the despised nonconformist. The Protestant churches and the public schools are no longer his allies. The respectable, upper middle-class citizen can no longer be safely counted upon to support abstinence."

The shift illustrates how communities resting on different bases can coalesce, and then separate and recombine in other ways. Protestantism and the middle class hold a rein still, as Gusfield views it. But it is an urban middle class to whom abstinence seems awkward. And presumably it is a Protestantism more resembling the original in this particular: one that can resume its drinking and view the temperance movement simply as a timed corrective to the hard-liquor explosion.

In view of all the foregoing, the drinking or abstinence of contemporary Americans may profitably be viewed against their communal ties and rivalries. This perspective assumes a double relevance if, as I proposed in the preceding chapter, the socially functional variety of drinking is a kind of drinking that is all about community anyway. The field study reported in this book has tried to bear all this in mind. Two adjoining boroughs on the fringe of the New York metropolitan region were chosen for study. Here, where diverse human streams mingle, I sought to learn how far people mingle alcohol in their mingling together.

If the local area seems to be of dwindling importance for generating community between moderns, it is only because the small region has been swallowed up in the larger one. The expression of the locality principle in the modern world is the nation. It is this that bounds the territory, the natural habitat, whose resources men exploit together. There is a romanticism which laments the passing of localism and tries to revive it, but I can hardly share in this. There is no point in regretting a man's indifference to Podunk when what has become of overwhelming importance for him is the fact that he is an American. Since the cooperative economic effort to which he contributes is not based on Podunk but America, the communal tie arising out of livelihood and the protection of livelihood is a national tie.

Of course, the sheer unmanageability of the large nations may eventually lead again to some kind of fragmentation. Some smaller area, possibly more like that of the states and provinces in North America now, may become the person's all-compelling community. That seems even more likely as the nations themselves merge into larger units, into communities of nations. The future is big with possibilities of that kind of decentralization, and it will be interesting to see what happens. Yet it seems certain that the size of any viable units will be decided by function. They will have to be large enough to embrace a highly diversified economy and produce sufficient wealth for all the services of a high civilization—things like universities and opera, for instance. They will scarcely be the urban or rural localities of past or present.

The functions of neighborhood and local government now are

the maintenance of some restricted services that are best supplied on a local basis. They are not so comprehensive or vital to a person that his sustenance and survival seem to rest on them, except insofar as they are tied into the national effort. They are therefore not charged with the same community significance as the national effort. If the present study purports to be a community study, it is in the sense I am laboring: it is made in full awareness of the fact that the sustenance that is sought from community flows in fact from affinity bonds. If a local area was selected for sampling, it was to tap the variety of communal bonds existing there.

COMMUNITIES IN GREENTOWN AND WILLOWDALE

The two boroughs examined in this study are in a still semirural New Jersey county lying in the New York-Philadelphia conurbation. It is in one of the outer rings of counties that the Regional Plan Association includes in the New York Metropolitan Region (18). Greentown is the County seat and is a comfortable commuting distance from New York. Transportation is now via the network of roads, including State and Federal highways; the two boroughs and the industrial plants in and around them have easy access to these. Greentown also has rail connections with Philadelphia and New York.

Of the employed people who live in the two boroughs, 82% work within the County. It is said that New York commuting is not nearly as common in Greentown today as it was in the past. More people find employment in manufacturing than in any of the major branches of employment used by the Census.[1] Within the two boroughs themselves more jobs are open in manufacturing; trade, which holds second place, offers less than a third as many jobs. But the larger industrial plants lie outside these boroughs. Several of these plants employ as many as 3000 or 4000 people. To man all of the County's industry requires that some workers commute into it, and more than a third of its work force does this. The area has

---

[1] These branches are designated as mining; construction; manufacturing; railway service; other transportation; communication, utilities and sanitary service; wholesale trade; eating and drinking places; other retail trade; business and repair services; private households; other personal services; hospitals; educational services; other professional and related services; public administration; other industries.

become a center for the production of chemical products and building materials; in addition there is manufacturing in pharmaceuticals, clothing, electronics and industrial equipment.

The importance of the kin group for moderns, in comparison with its importance earlier, is harder to guess at than the changing importance of the residential area. Studies are contradicting the stereotype of a kin group nearly defunct. It is still very much alive and depended on. But two things have dealt it a blow and industry is one of them: industry, that is, integrated on a national basis. Since industry demands highly specialized competences, it interposes an advanced and specialized education between parents and their children. After this, as likely as not, it will interpose great geographical and social distances, as the children move away to the work for which they have been fitted and as they move into a different lifestyle.

The second blow to the kin group is from the political norm of equality: It is opposed to privilege and wants no child to have advantages over another by the mere fact of birth. So it is hard to maintain a kin solidarity in wealth and prestige: every man is the maker of his own fortune. The family and wider kin group feel under ruthless pressure at times: to procreate and populate, to support the children in many ways, but to let them go and, indeed, send them forth to where the jobs are—across the world if need be. What we choose to call "ethnic groups" are the colonies of one nation in another whose industry has been magnetic enough to burst the kin bonds of the first. For the ethnic bond is essentially a national bond operating anachronistically.

1. Ethnic and Racial Communities

As with all the New Jersey counties located in the outer ring of the New York metropolitan region, the county's population has grown continually since 1870. The two boroughs, specifically, have shown an increase in every Census. Greentown had 4800 persons in 1900; 12,500 in 1960; Willowdale increased in the same interval from 3200 to 6100. A prodigious 30-year increase has been predicted for the County as a whole from 1955 to 1985 (35). Population is expected to multiply by 5 and jobs by 4.

As well as increasing, the population of the area has continually diversified (Table 1). The region now making up Greentown and Willowdale was settled at the end of the 17th century predominantly by English, Scottish and Dutch people. The Census data from 1870 onward give evidence of several distinct migrations into the County: (1) from Ireland, already by 1870; (2) from Austria, between 1890 and 1900, and from Hungary, between 1890 and 1910; (3) from Germany, between 1870 and 1950; (4) from Italy, between 1890 and 1930; (5) from Russia, between 1890 and 1920; (6) from Scotland, between 1920 and 1930; (7) from Poland, between 1900 and 1930; (8) from Czechoslovakia, between 1910 and 1930.

Negroes, who at present comprise about one-twelfth of Greentown's population but are absent from Willowdale, came early. In 1680 there were slaves in New Jersey; by 1790 there were 2000 slaves in the County and the adjoining one.

It is difficult to trace the nationality background of the present population of the two boroughs and it could be quite misleading to rely on the most recent Census for data on "foreign stock." For this is simply a count of persons who were themselves born in other countries or had parents born there. For instance, observers often remark that "most of the inhabitants of Willowdale seem to be Italian," and it is probably true that many more are of Italian descent than the 1850 (out of 6100)

TABLE 1.—*Population of Greentown and Willowdale by Nativity and Parentage, in Per Cent*

Foreign Stock (i.e., persons born in other countries or having a parent or parents born there)	Greentown (N=3900)	Willowdale (N=3000)	Total (N=6900)
United Kingdom	12	1	8
Ireland	5	2	3
Norway	<1	<1	<1
Sweden	1	<1	1
Germany	8	5	7
Poland	13	7	10
Czechoslovakia	4	9	6
Austria	6	5	6
Hungary	2	3	3
Russia	9	3	6
Italy	23	61	40
Canada	2	1	2
Mexico	1	0	<1
All other and not reported	14	3	9
Native Born of Native Parents	(N=8600)	(N=3100)	(N=11,700)
White	87	100	90
Negro	13	0	9
All other races	1	0	<1
Total Population	12,500	6100	18,600

who are counted in the 1960 Census as "foreign stock." This Census shows, however, what are the freshest major sources of population supply from outside. In Greentown these are, in order of size, Italy, Poland, the United Kingdom and Germany; in Willowdale they are Italy and (a long way behind) Poland and Czechoslovakia. The Census also shows that about half of the Willowdale people and nearly a third of the Greentown people are recent enough in their arrival to be designated "foreign stock": they or their parents were born outside of America.

Table 1 shows the population by nativity and parentage in the two boroughs.

2. Class Communities

The racial and ethnic diversity of the two boroughs is matched by a social-class diversity that is not unconnected with it. Both boroughs have workers in all occupational categories of the Census. Table 2-A shows the percentage of all workers in five selected job categories. In both places craftsmen and operatives (counted together) make the largest group, although they constitute a considerably larger proportion in Willowdale. In Greentown professional and managerial jobs (counted together) make a close second; in Willowdale this category, though sizable, is smaller. In both boroughs clerical and sales workers constitute a third major group. The number of service workers and laborers is small. If we distinguish between mental and manual occupations and separate them by a line between sales workers and craftsmen, slightly more than half of Greentown's workers (51%) are in mental occupations, and a slightly larger proportion of Willowdale's (59%) are in the manual trades. In comparison with the national totals Greentown has more workers in the professional and managerial category, Willowdale more in the category of craftsmen and operatives.

TABLE 2.—*Occupation and Income, in Per Cent*

A. *Workers in a Selection* (*not exhaustive*) *of Job Categories*

	Greentown (N=5352)	Willowdale (N=2565)	All U.S.A. (N=64,639,247)
Professional, technical & managers, officials and proprietors except farm	27	17	20
Clerical and sales	24	20	22
Craftsmen, foremen & operatives	29	46	32
Service except private household	8	7	8
Laborers except farm	4	6	5

B. *Family Incomes*

	(N=3278)	(N=1611)	(N=45,128,393)
<$5000	21	21	42
$5000 to $9999	53	63	43
$10,000+	26	16	15

Family incomes in both boroughs range from under $1000 to $10,000 and over. Table 2-B shows that the same proportion in the two boroughs have family incomes below $5000 and that the greater proportion in both boroughs receive between $5000 and $10,000. In Greentown 10% more than in Willowdale have incomes of $10,000 or above. In comparison with the national totals there are more higher incomes. It was estimated in 1962 that half the income earned by Greentown residents was earned by one-quarter of the households, while another quarter received only 7.3% of the total earned (data from Willowdale were not published).

Difference in income and life style attaching to difference in occupation can engender divergent political sympathies. Selected elections in the years 1960 through 1963 showed consistent majority votes for Democratic candidates in Willowdale and for Republican candidates in Greentown, with a still greater Republican majority in the surrounding township. It was common to find a slight Democratic majority in those election districts of Greentown which include the Negro and working-class populations.

Segregation by class is a real segregation here as in other places. People with more advantages procure themselves better homes in better neighborhoods. The Census analysis of labor-force characteristics shows one of Willowdale's two census tracts and one of Greentown's four to have the higher concentrations of workers of less skill and training. Five well-informed Willowdale citizens and six from Greentown gave judgments about their borough's population dispersion. They agreed that the northwest corner of Willowdale has the more prosperous people, the southwest corner of town those of middle income, the southeast corner below the railroad track those of lower income. They also reported that the central portion of town south of the railroad has mostly people of Italian descent, the area directly east of it, "Slavics." In Greentown the better-off people were seen to reside again in the northwest corner, people of lower income to be concentrated south of the main street, but also resided through the remainder of the town with the people of middle income. Concentrations of immigrant groups could not be identified in Greentown. The Negro population was concentrated in two neighborhoods: the lower-income area and a neighborhood in the northwest of town, east of and rather like an annex to the upper-income area. About 100 Negroes live in the town.

3. Religious Communities

Nothing can be learned about the religious diversity of the locality from the U.S. Census, since it scrupulously avoids questioning on this. Greentown has 17 places of worship, Willowdale 5. Greentown's are mostly Protestant and comprise 3 Reformed churches, 2 Baptist, and 1 each of the following: Methodist, Lutheran, Episcopal, Reformed Episcopal, African Methodist, Episcopal Zion, Assembly of God, Shiloh Pentecostal, Christian Scientist and Roman Catholic. There are, besides, Orthodox, Conservative and Reformed Jewish congregations. Willowdale has 3 Catholic churches and a Reformed and Lutheran church.

The leaders of the various congregations supplied information on the size of their memberships (Table 3-A). Membership, however, is reckoned differently in the different sects. To the Roman Catholics, for instance, it means residence within the parish boundary; to the Baptists it means profession of faith. Each church can also draw a haul of membership from outside the borough limits. This is particularly true of the Roman Catholic churches whose parish boundaries extend past the boroughs. The different sects also impose differing requirements on their members if they are to give satisfacton as "active members," and information on members' activeness (as their leaders viewed it) and on attendance at worship was also obtained (Tables 3-B and 3-C).

Of the 22,345 members of churches in the two boroughs, 16,007 were Catholics and 1040 Jews (650 Orthodox, 240 Conservative, 150 Reformed). The 5298 Protestants were divided as follows: Reformed, 1512, Methodist, 960, Lutheran, 860, Episcopal, 700, Baptist, 627, Shiloh Pentecostal, 300, African Methodist Episcopal, 140, Reformed Episcopal, 98, Christian Science, 65, Assembly of God, 36.

The fact that the number of church members exceeds the total population of the two boroughs reflects the extent to which membership is

TABLE 3.—*Religious Membership and Attendance*

A. *Number of Centers of Worship*
   Having Each Size of Membership

	Protestant	Catholic	Jewish	Totals
5000+	0	2	0	2
1000-4999	0	2	0	2
500-999	5	0	1	6
300-499	3	0	1	4
100-299	4	0	1	5
<100	3	0	0	3
Totals	15	4	3	22

B. *Percentage of Whole Membership*
   Acknowledged to be Active

	Protestant	Catholic	Jewish	Totals
<70%	5	0	2	7
70%+	10	4	1	15
Totals	15	4	3	22

C. *Percentage of Whole Membership*
   Attending Workshop Regularly

	Protestant	Catholic	Jewish	Totals
<50%	8	4	3	15
50%+	7	0	0	7
Totals	15	4	3	22

drawn from outside. There is no quick way of knowing what precise numbers of the population under study profess adherence to each branch of religion. In the case of Protestantism, large numbers do this without registering church membership at all. But to have a count is not of the greatest importance. It is clear from the data that the locality studied is the center for Protestant, Catholic and Jewish communities, all of which are large enough to be publicly influential.

Chapter 3

The Shadow of The Past

THIS AREA of New Jersey was opened up sufficiently long ago for it to have seen something of neighborhood community in the old sense at its beginning. The settlers who came in from Long Island and other parts of the state of New York at the end of the 17th century made a farming community that was largely self-sufficient. They grew their own grain, burnt their own lime, tanned their own leather, did their own carpentry and mill-wrighting, made their own footwear and clothing, and produced their own beer, cider and spirits. By 1699, the First Reformed Church of Willowdale was in existence. People in meeting there affirmed their unity—as they also did, incidentally, at the taverns. Besides being places to obtain refreshment and lodging, taverns then were places where a more dispersed population would meet to prattle when they came to town, where they would go to learn the news of the day or do business, and would even convene public meetings. The tavern keepers were respected men of unusual influence, highly informed in public affairs. Besides expressing ingroup unity, the taverns stood as expressions of hospitality to the outsider whose travel brought him into the neighborhood. The most historic of these taverns was that of Cornelius Tunison, which is known to have been in operation around 1769. In 1781, for instance, a meeting of freeholders and justices was held there for the purpose of raising money to build a new jail. Where two main roads intersected, the village of Greentown grew up, and Tunison's Tavern was the hub of much of its business. The County Hotel, which dominates one approach to the town, occupies the site now.

SOCIAL DISORDER, INTEMPERANCE AND REVIVALISM
IN THE 18TH CENTURY

There is no reason to think the early drinking patterns of New Jersey or of this particular area along the Willow River were much different from those of the other colony states, and there is evidence that it underwent the same transformations in the 18th and 19th centuries. Though distilled spirits were not unknown, beer and wine, supplemented by some brandy and cider, were the principal beverages at first. For persons of Dutch ancestry beer was especially important. Drinking at this time seems to have been decorous enough: the most moral and religious of this predominantly Protestant people appear to have cherished it. But Mellick (24), who has recorded much social history of the County, sees an agency of intemperance to be already abroad in the country when the area was being settled (24, p. 614): "The great impetus to intemperance came in about 1640 with the introduction of West India rum, and in this country sixty years later intoxicants were powerfully reinforced by the beginning of the manufacture of Medford and other rums by puritan New England."

The popular adoption of rum as a beverage in the area is attributed by Mellick, as it is also by Voorhees (36), to the various wars of the 18th century, especially those of 1756 and 1776. They believed that, as the troops were allotted rations of rum and thereby learned to depend on it, they carried the practice of drinking it into their homes and communities.

The 18th century as a whole was a time when the social structure was shaken both in Europe and the New World. Conditions that might dispose to what in Chapter 1 I have called assuagement drinking were widespread. While we lack precise measures which could identify it as being that, the accounts of much of the drinking of the time suggest that it was. It was a reaction to demoralization on the part of socially dislocated persons who could not expect to repeat their ancestors' pattern of life, but who did not know what they could expect in its place. In marked contrast to this reaction was the revivalism that came out in much of the religion of the time: the Evangelical Revival in England and the Great Awakening in America took place then. Yet, this can be viewed as an alternative response to the same social conditions. The moral stiffening of a resurgent puritanism was another side of that response. For when the supports of a stable social structure are down, men seek by way of compensation to feel effective "inwardly." Yet they divide over how this is to be done. Some resort to immediate physical gratifications like assuagement drinking or assuagement sex, others to immediate spiritual gratifications.

Since assuagement drinking and the religion of experience are competing answers to the inadequacy of human society, there is enmity between them. It is when society is greatly shaken that its inadequacies cause more anguish, of course; but it is always inadequate to some degree. For this reason revivalist religion keeps alerted for the outbreak of assuagement drinking and it will then, if necessary, justify abstinence. It does so on the grounds that where there is even a risk of that abuse occurring, drinking is best avoided. It adopts the principle that it is better to enter into life maimed than to have two hands or two feet and be cast into Hell. The religion of experience does seem to be recoiling from Hell itself, however dimly it discerns it there, in assuagement practices. Hell is not a place any more than Heaven is. But its unquenchable fires are expressive symbolism for insatiability. And it could be that it is those who, being socially dislocated, have no heavenly city either, that are symbolized by the lost.

The religion of experience does not accept it as a matter of indifference whether demoralized men are further "lost" by being filled with wine or "saved" by being filled with the Spirit. In its eyes the former constitutes despair; only the latter is a constructive response leading to social reconstruction. It is also an observable fact that it was out of the latter response that the first stirrings of various reform movements came in the second part of the 18th century, bent on changing the conditions that had kept people from being members of one another for so long. The temperance movement was only one of the more influential of them.

It has been fashionable, ever since Prohibition proved unpopular and failed, to make the pioneers of temperance look slightly ridiculous. But it was they who responded to an appalling challenge of their day when millions around them were beaten by it. This must be acknowledged and can be done without necessarily applauding all that came from what they did. Nothing could be more a caricature of the early temperance reformers than to make them out straightlaced and interfering prigs who tried to stop people having a good time. They were simply citizens accepting responsibility for a problem they could hardly understand. Restrained drinking was their aim, not abstinence or prohibition; and they expected that it might be furthered by having people pledge against the drinking of distilled spirits. If the movement they launched produced an excess of virtue in producing Prohibition, that was because it got momentum from reacting to a serious social problem.

The sources of the great social dislocations of the 18th century were the industrial and agricultural revolutions which made the patterns of life in town and country obsolete, the vast growth and movement of population, the new classes and the new governments that implemented the will of the classes that came to dominance, and the international alliances and rivalries of these new governments. It was an unrest that produced both the American and French Revolutions and did not subside till the Napoleonic Wars were over.

It was doubtless because it was such a period of bad feeling that the era that saw recovery in sight, so far as America was concerned (1816-1824), came to be called the "era of good feeling." It is a somewhat unfortunate coincidence that in that period of demoralization, and constituting one of its minor technological advances in fact, efficient ways of distilling commercially were first devised. For the first time in history anyone could purchase distilled spirits and could get as much as he could drink for very little money. The London ginshop sign epitomized the situation dramatically: "DRUNK FOR A HALF-PENNY: DEAD DRUNK FOR A PENNY." It was whisky production that swelled the supply in America, and by the early 19th century it had supplanted rum as the popular spirit.

Various observers, without having any moralizing intent, agree in their reports on overdrinking in widely separated parts of America during the 18th century and, indeed, well into the 19th. For, although Monroe's "era of good feeling" ushered in a new stability, the drinking habits of the era preceding could not be extinguished so suddenly. And change now had more than habit to overcome: excess had added to itself the sanction of the superstition that spirits were good for health and strengthening. Even Carson's book (6), which otherwise reads like an advertisement for whisky, concedes that there was a "dark age of American drinking." Carson summarizes some of the reporting on it (6, *pp. 67-68*):

"A meal at a house of public entertainment cost a quarter without whiskey or thirty-seven and a half cents *with*. An account book of an old inn in Potosi, Missouri, sets forth clear evidence that the patrons preferred the thirty-seven-and-a-half-cent deal. Running a doggery was a good way for a man with political aspirations to keep himself in the public eye, meanwhile getting his personal liquor at wholesale prices. Many who hoped to feed from the public trough availed themselves of this method of advancement and refreshment.

"The moderate or occasional social drinker seems not to have existed. Men drank to excess or not at all. This sharp cleavage makes the per capita consumption of distilled spirits all the more impressive. Rising gradually from the level of about two and a half gallons in the closing years of the eighteenth century, the figure reached an all-time high in 1860 of three and a quarter gallons. Statistically everybody is included: women, children, slaves, Indians, John B. Gough, the temperance orator, who made a profession out of describing his feats in tippling traps, the man who took one glass of elderberry wine on New Year's Eve, as well as the hero of the old ditty:

> He is not drunk who from the floor
> Can rise again, and drink once more,
> But he is drunk, who prostrate lies,
> And cannot drink and cannot rise.

"Since an average is an arithmetical mean, the drinking population somewhere, possibly in California, was doing even better. In San Francisco there was a barroom for every one hundred inhabitants. Here beer and bourbon fought a Homeric battle for the throats of the thin line of patriots who balanced on the city's brass rails. In Albany, New York, the Dutch demonstrated that they had hard heads by putting away ten gallons of the American schnapps for every inhabitant. Sadly, Samuel Dexter, President of the Massachusetts Society for the Suppression of Intemperance, observed, 'The rocket-flask is grown into a case-bottle and the keg into a barrel.' And all the while the settlements pushed west, the population doubled and redoubled, and the drovers, traders, boatmen, exchange brokers and one-gallus land agents, the quarter-race crowd with their dirks and their thirst, could agree as they raised a glass of the ardent, 'Yes, sir, we air an Almighty people.'"

If I have written somewhat cryptically of a "hard-liquor explosion," it was to this I was referring. It was felt in this particular area of New Jersey as much as anywhere. Mellick (24, *p. 619*) has written:

"It is Voorhees who has left us observations on the . . . area itself. He asserted that children grew up there in the vice of intemperance, taught by their parents to love spirits. Of [the] County he reported that 'drunkenness was like the destroying angel that passed over the land of Egypt—there was scarcely a house where it did not leave one dead.' During this period it was found more profitable to plant orchards in order that the fruit might be converted into cider and that into spirits. In the township . . . by the beginning of the nineteenth century, there existed eight or more distilleries and the price of cider spirits became so reduced that it was sold from twenty-five to thirty cents per gallon. The evil continued to increase to an alarming degree until 1820 when it seemed to roll onward like an overwhelming torrent. . . . The bottle was the companion alike of the wealthy and fashionable and the destitute, humble and obscure."

It is of interest that the area was not without its own spiritual warfare to counter this threatening drift. Theodorus J. Freylinghuysen came from Holland to take up duty as pastor to the Willowdale church in 1720. He came preaching the evangelical doctrine of the necessity of a new heart. In this, it appears, he was more a prophet discerning the need of his time than an exemplar of the austere tradition within his church. For clergymen of his own denomination and some of his own church elders opposed him. He was accused of "enthusiasm" and it was said that he departed from the order and usages of the church. Freylinghuysen claimed his doctrine was that of the Reformation and of the church of the Netherlands especially. He braved his opponents' wrath and followed where he felt led, converting many persons in the 27 or more years of his ministry. This was recognized as a kind of little revival of the area. Freylinghuysen's work was known to Whitefield and Jonathan Edwards, who were the principal figures in the American Great Awakening. The Willowdale revival, along with some other local revivals in New England, made a kind of prologue to the Great Awakening; and Freylinghuysen was a kind of morning star to it (26, *pp. 159-204*).

SOCIAL RECONSTRUCTION, ABSTINENCE AND REFORM IN THE 19TH CENTURY

Recognition for pioneering temperance is generally given to two Presbyterians, one a physician, Dr. Benjamin Rush of Philadelphia, the other a clergyman, the Reverend Lyman Beecher of New England.[1] These men played a decisive role in formulating opinion and initiating inquiry into the effects of alcohol, and it is significant that this contribution came out of an intellectual tradition like Presbyterianism. But the Quakers and Methodists, each inheritors of a

[1] Beecher's role has recently been described by Winkler (40).

revivalism that stressed inward strength, had already expressed moral concern in action. In all cases, however, the concern was over the effects of distilled spirits. In 1787, the Society of Friends passed a resolution recommending that its members should not buy or sell spirituous liquors; the Wesleyan Discipline of 1753 had done the same. Rush wrote his influential discourses on spirits in 1778 and 1784. Beecher took up temperance work against spirits around about 1811.

One of the most interesting features of the 19th-Century movement to restore temperance was the way organizations sprang up with this as their special purpose. Though largely inspired and supported by church people, the aim was specific enough to be furthered apart from the church. While a group appeared in Moreau, New York, in 1808 and the Massachusetts Society for the Suppression of Intemperance began in 1813, it was mainly in the second quarter of the 19th century that the organizations burgeoned. National societies promoted local branches, and Voorhees (36) reported that around 1835 temperance associations were established in most of the neighborhoods along the Willow River. They appear to have made some kind of impact. In 1873 he wrote:

"Decanters were removed from sideboards and banished from social circles. Hay and harvest gatherings, building raising, burials of the dead, marriages, and entertainments for friends were all had without the use of intoxicating liquors. More recently tavern bars have been closed on the Sabbath Day and days of election. In the township referred to, where there were eight distilleries in operation in 1800, there is not one at the present time."

We may presume that not all of this was accomplished by a pledge to avoid spirits alone. For a transition from that understanding of temperance to total abstinence occurred in the movement between 1836 and 1850. The change did not come without opposition and it is hard to trace the reason for it. There is a tendency in any reform movement for moderates to be superseded by radicals and it may have been simply a case of this. Yet that tendency can sometimes be forced by necessity, if change is to come at all. In this instance it might be that a more complete break from alcohol proved necessary if people steeped in excess were to be helped or controlled.

Just as excess in the 18th century has to be seen as part of a general social disorder, temperance and abstinence in the 19th century have to be viewed as part of a general social reconstruction. In a number of ways people evinced a new willingness to embrace a yoke of strictness for the sake of the common good. Morale was improving as, by cooperative effort, men and women mastered the novelties that had proved overwhelming a century before. That morale was expressed in America in the ways that *community* is always expressed.[2] There was a determination to face public issues and resolve them, ultimately by the binding legislation of the political authority. Industrial enterprise and reform movements showed an awareness that the social institutions are what common consent makes them. There was a resurgence of mutual help and an efflorescence of culture.

The chrysalis of order was growing in chaos with the birth of the nation in the late 18th and first half of the 19th century. The political developments were paralleled by a vast industrial expansion. America became a world power and began developing its own cultural resources. And running parallel to all this were diverse reform movements. They expressed the same confidence in the worthwhileness of working together to improve things, all to make a great nation. They are evidence that the era continuing into the first two decades of this century reached something like a high-water mark of civilization, in the sense in which I have been using the term. There was an abundant surplus for supererogatory works. Besides the reform effort directed toward drinking, there were efforts directed toward emancipation, citizenship and franchise for Negroes, rights and suffrage for women, improved conditions for labor, greater welfare for children, the conservation and fuller exploitation of natural resources, and public hygiene. Private philanthropy supported humanitarian and educational causes.

From being the whole end of special-purpose organizations, the time came when temperance (usually now understood as abstinence) was made one of the several aims of social and fraternal organizations. The Sons of Temperance, founded in 1842, is typical of these. The mutual aid expressed in these movements, of course, bespeaks the high pitch of community existing. It was in these

[2] I have given an itemization of the separate aspects of community elsewhere (10, *pp. 106-107*).

associations that prohibition as a feasible goal was conceived and nurtured. One of them, the International Order of Good Templars, inspired the formation of the National Prohibition Party and supplied some precedents for the Woman's Christian Temperance Union and the Anti-Saloon League. I suggest that the reason for this was that abstinence itself had become part of the adornment of life which these people cherished as distinctive of them. Their leisure, their entertaining, their dignity and grace, the manners of their elite, were as much marked by avoidance of alcohol as these have been marked at other times by its use. To protect this pattern of life and extend it, it seemed natural to use what power they had to bring in prohibition by political means. Especially since, when the sense of community is strong, it is felt that the political authority can be entrusted with much.

Nor, apparently, was it very difficult to legislate prohibition in many places. National Prohibition was but the culmination of a third wave of prohibitory activity on the part of many separate states. The Woman's Christian Temperance Union, though effective in influencing opinion, consolidated sentiments already widespread. More important, the Anti-Saloon League operated to concentrate the power of the supporters of a hundred temperance organizations by giving them a political program to endorse: it even presented itself as "the church in action against the saloon." Yet continued drinking and popular opposition to Prohibition soon culminated in its repeal in almost every state where it was adopted. Although many felt action against drinking to be imperative, Prohibition, when tried, did not appear to be effective.

The irony and, indeed, the poignancy in prohibition is that it came precisely at the time when men and women were once again ready to give symbolic expression to an achieved community. They could well have taken hold of alcohol then and used it ornamentally to express their trust—in a way that might have been impossible a century before. A drastic measure prompted by the assuagement drinking of a century before was only just devised—excruciatingly out of time. It was a case of *lag*. It was the kind of thing T. S. Eliot[3] refers to:

[3] *Gerontion,* lines 34–46.

History has many cunning passages, contrived corridors
And issues, deceives with whispering ambitions,
Guides us by vanities. Think now
She gives when our attention is distracted
And what she gives, gives with such supple confusions
That the giving famishes the craving. Gives too late
What's not believed in, or is still believed,
In memory only reconsidered passion. Gives too soon
Into weak hands, what's thought can be dispensed with
Till the refusal propagates a fear. Think
Neither fear nor courage saves us. Unnatural vices
Are fathered by our heroism. Virtues
Are forced upon us by our impudent crimes.

Yet that lag would hardly have gone so unresisted if there had not been the added factor of lowered discrimination in judgment and, as a consequence of it, of confusion in meaning. If drinking has to be categorically outlawed because many abuse it, the impression can be left that all drinking is an abuse: certainly such an inference is drawn. That there might possibly be a kind of drinking that has an ornamental meaning can then be forgotten. This is a first eclipse of meaning in drinking. Yet to be later permitted by Repeal to do what has been forbidden, can then be construed as an invitation to license. This is a second eclipse of meaning, a compounding of distortions. It is a crucial problem of this study to ask what sense of meaningfulness in drinking has been recovered by modern Americans in view of this history. It seems not impossible, if the compounded distortions I allude to did occur, that meaningfulness in drinking would only be recovered after a time of searching. Two little news comments on drinking at Repeal betray a certain tentativeness, a groping and lack of assurance, both in drinkers and observers. There is also a hint that assurance was being sought by return to the familiar pattern of hard-liquor consumption.

The front page of the *Somerset Messenger Gazette*, of 8 December 1933, reported "WHAT THEY ARE DRINKING":

"The drinking habit of the thirteen years of prohibition has changed somewhat according to the reports from the restaurants and hotels in New York. Old retainers in prominent hotels looked somewhat puzzled as they accepted repeated orders for hard drinks. Although the best domestic wines, some of them aged since before prohibition, and the finest vintages of France and Italy were available in many resorts, the overwhelming majority of orders were for highballs, cocktails and 'straight drinks.'"

On 2 January 1934 the same paper carried the headline, "VICIN-ITY'S FIRST NEW YEAR'S REVEL SINCE REPEAL MERRY BUT ORDERLY." The column said that the area—

"in company with the rest of the United States outdid itself in tying a tin can to 1933. . . . Last year's requiem was echoed by laughter, merriment and the gurgling sounds of more liquid nourishment of the alcoholic type than ever flowed since old John Barleycorn was in his prime. There were few parties of a public nature hereabouts this year outside of the various night clubs. . . . The great majority of folks took their new cheer home, and lights were in the windows of many dwellings until dawn. Confectioners reported a run on ginger ale."

Chapter 4

Opening a Window on the Present

THE INTERVIEW SAMPLE AND METHODOLOGY

SINCE the study depended on sampling the community ties existing, and since the location of persons party to them was not known in advance and could be different for each tie, taking a random sample of households was the procedure indicated. Such a sample was drawn and the households contacted. But randomness was not achieved because of the high proportion of losses.[1]

Composition of the Sample

There are few indices which would help us to know whether eligible cases who did not participate were of one type, or even of several types, and whether it was for systematic or random reasons that they were excluded. Of the 312 households that proved eligible for inclusion, occupants of 6 were known to be out of town during the period of the interviewing and another 25 occupants could not be contacted after frequent calls. Therefore, 281 households having occupants available were approached (June-September 1964); cooperation was secured from 152 of them, i.e., from 54%. These households contained the 321 interviewed persons (at the visit of 2 hours or more all persons living together who were of high-school age or above were interviewed). Assuming that the population aged 15 or over was roughly our target, this yield made 2.5% of the 1960 Census count. The number comprised: 234 residents of Greentown, 87 of Willowdale; 177 women, 144 men; 279 persons aged 21 or over, 42 under 21; 272 householders or wives of same, 49 children of householders; 245 drinkers, 76 abstainers.

Nothing we know concerning those who declined to take part or their reasons for doing so would lead us to think they represented special types of people. In particular, there is no reason to think they exemplified any special position in relation to drinking: abstainers rather than drinkers, for instance, or heavy drinkers rather than light. For never during the approach was the study presented as having any special concern with drinking at all. The questions, it was said, would deal with various live public issues, and drinking and nondrinking was mentioned as one

---

[1] It might be better to offer payment to interviewees in studies of this depth, but in this instance that was not done.

37

among others. The reasons for nonparticipation most frequently given were lack of interest, lack of time, not wanting to get involved, illness in the family.[2]

The Polk Directory was used to compile a list of all dwelling units in the two boroughs. The dwelling units were numbered from 1 to 6000 in the order in which they appeared in the Directory and a sample of 300 households was selected, using a table of random numbers. Another 50 were drawn to compensate for losses. Of the 350 households, 16 had not been approached when the field interviewing had to be terminated, leaving 334. Upon investigation by the interviewers, 22 of those proved to be "dummies": unoccupied dwellings, business premises, no such address, and so on. This left the 312 correctly identified residences that were eligible for inclusion.

Interviewing

In the first week of June 1964, a letter was addressed to the occupant of each dwelling unit selected from the Directory. In that week also the study was announced in a news column of the local newspaper. While these were probably the first intimations most people received, the projected study had been announced to some of the leading citizens at a public dinner the previous year. In the interval after that dinner a number of people holding public office in the boroughs had been asked to cooperate in supplying background information. The bulk of the interviewing was completed between 6 June and the end of July. During August and September, when two additional interviewers were available, it was possible to have the remainder completed.

The interviewers were not professional sociologists. While a few were graduate students in sociology, most of them were mature-aged men or women with some training or occupational experience which, it was presumed, would dispose them to this kind of work. They attended a series of 3 training sessions prior to going into the field. Here they were acquainted with the nature of the study and some of the ideas behind it. General interviewing techniques were discussed and specific instructions given on use of the interviewing schedule. Initially there were 27 interviewers and, when engaged, each was asked to aim at completing interviews with the occupants of at least 10 households. The number of interviewers approaching and completing interviews with different numbers of households is given in Table 4.

While the introductory letter had gone out from Rutgers University, it was the interviewers who made the approach to the respondents to

[2] Comparisons of the responses of the interviewed sample with those in the national survey by Cahalan, Cisin and Crossley (5) indicate that for the most part the interviewees in the present study were sufficiently similar to support the impression that they represent a fairly typical American community.

TABLE 4.—*Households Approached and Interviews Completed*

Number of Interviewers	Number of Households Approached	Total	Number of Interviewers	Interviews Completed	Total
2	17	34	1	10	10
4	16	64	3	9	27
2	15	30	1	8	8
6	14	84	3	7	21
3	13	39	5	6	30
1	12	12	7	5	35
2	11	22	1	4	4
5	10	50	5	3	15
1	8	8	1	2	2
1	7	7	2	0	0
1	6	6			
1	3	3			
Totals					
29		359*	29		152

*This total exceeds by 25 the total number of households approached. This is because the two late-arriving interviewers reapproached households that were approached previously but not previously enlisted.

enlist their cooperation. The interviewing itself was such as to tax their skill and ingenuity. What they were called upon to do was something like administering a questionnaire to a small group. The respondents were asked, as far as possible, to fill out their own schedules, the interviewer acting as interpreter and guide according to the needs of each. As the sample included people of different levels of education and sophistication, the interviewers were asked to be prepared to interpret the schedule. My aim was not to standardize the administration of the schedule but to be sure that each respondent had understood it in terms that were meaningful to himself. On occasion, where the respondent found writing difficult, the interviewer did the recording. Copies of the interview schedule and notes on the indices can be obtained from the National Auxiliary Publications Service.[3]

Data Analysis

The data were coded and put on cards for computer analysis. Much of the coding was intricate, sometimes composite indices were used, and numerous tables resulted. It is not appropriate to clutter up the present work by reproducing the entire set of tables. In the following text, therefore, I usually refer only to those data which are relevant to the context

[3] To obtain the Interview Schedule and Notes on the Indices, order NAPS Document No. 02227 from ASIS/NAPS, c/o Microfiche Publications, 305 East 46 St., New York, NY 10017; remit with order $1.50 for microfilm copy, $7.70 for full-size photocopy.

of discussion. But, where required, there will be a reference to a table showing the whole set of data from which they are drawn. (The total number of cases will vary for different items because every question did not apply to every case and some responses were ambiguous and therefore unclassifiable.)

Numerous cross-tabulations were made. Wherever these suggested the presence of meaningful relationships, they are reported. At times cells of an original table have been collapsed in order to have sufficient cases with which to make comparison. But this has only been done where the scores in the cells being combined were in the same direction originally, and where it made sense to combine the cells because they were similar. The tables give the statistical significance of relationships found. Many more cross-tabulations were made than will receive mention. It was disappointing that the findings of many of them were inconclusive because of the small number of cases in some of the cells. One particularly disappointing limitation was imposed by the small numbers: Since the total number of persons under age 21 was not great enough to comprise a sample in itself, and since the distribution of their responses was not significantly different from that of persons over 21, they cannot be treated separately in the analysis.

The data to be reported fall into two main divisions, corresponding to Chapters 5 and 6 of this book. In Chapter 5 actual practices in regard to drinking and abstinence and the person's attitudes to these are reported. Then in Chapter 6 the general ideals that the person has to guide him in orienting himself in these areas of action are dealt with. Finally, in Chapter 7, the findings are related to the larger questions raised in the first part of the book.

Since this study was designed and completed, the results of a U.S. national survey of drinking practices have been published by Cahalan, Cisin and Crossley (5).[4] Where possible, the national distributions have been compared with the local distributions of the present study. The comparisons may not always be precise, since the same set of questions was not asked. For instance, there is a rudimentary discrepancy in that Cahalan, Cisin and Crossley classify anyone who drinks less frequently than once a year an "abstainer," whereas I mean by this anyone who categorically refuses to drink. In their study and by their definition, 32% are "abstainers," in my study and by my definition, 24%. Even though the studies are not precisely matched, certain broad comparisons are possible. Since in all instances there is a general correspondence between the findings, no comment is needed, the correspondence being accepted as confirmation.

[4] Hereinafter referred to as "the national survey."

Chapter 5

Individual Choice
and Social Sanction

M OST OF THE PEOPLE questioned in this study took a definite
stance on the practice of drinking and were divided fairly
evenly in their general disposition toward it: 43% laid greater stress
on its desirable aspect, 49% on its undesirable aspect (1% were
ambivalent, 5% stressed neither aspect, and 2% were unclassified).
[In the national survey 78% reported that drinking did more harm
than good (5, *pp. 131-132*).] Asked why they viewed the practice
of drinking as they did, 27% of those stressing its desirable aspect
reported that it was relaxing, 19% that it was intrinsically pleasur-
able, 16% that it was an aid to sociability; 21% replied that, although abuses could occur with alcohol, it was always possible
to avoid them. Of those who stressed the undesirable aspect, 31%
gave as their reason the loss of control it could induce, possibly
with resulting accident, and 16% the possibility that habitual drinking might impair health and cause addiction; 13% reported that,
while alcohol might indeed be used without harm, the chances
were always greater that it would generate trouble.

PREDOMINANCE OF STRESS ON UNDESIRABLE ASPECT

It seems more appropriate to start with the difference among
respondents in over-all attitude than simply with the distinction
between "drinker" and "abstainer." For the difference in attitude
leaves us with quite a different impression, and what it indicates
is probably far more significant. Ordinarily, it is assumed that the
proportion of drinkers in the population indicates the proportion
of people who are "for it," the proportion of abstainers the proportion "against it." Yet in our sample, while only 24% were "abstainers" in the sense that they would categorically refuse a drink, 49%
laid greatest stress on the undesirable aspect of drinking—actually

6% more than the number that would stress the desirable aspect. [In the national survey 32% were abstainers, in the sense that they had not had a drink in the past year (5, *p. 14*).] Clearly, a large proportion of people who are not categorically unwilling to drink nevertheless view the practice mainly in its undesirable aspect. (There is possibly some connection between this fact and the unwillingness of many of these persons to be dubbed "drinkers." In interviewing them we were in the habit of calling them "drinkers," simply in order to distinguish them from the "abstainers" in the sample. But many of them said they found this practice repugnant.)

Four Relationships with Aspect Stressed

Cross-tabulations indicated four relationships with the tendency to stress one or other aspect. Persons in occupational category I of Hollingshead's occupational scale (i.e., higher executives, proprietors of large concerns, and major professionals) were more prone to stress the desirable aspect than persons in occupational category VII (unskilled employees) (Table 5-A). More of those who stressed the desirable aspect had memberships in voluntary groups with a socially unifying character, rather than in sectional and partisan groups (Table 5-B). With a decreasing frequency in religious observance there was an increasing incidence of stressing the desirable aspect (Table 5-C). Although the differences were not great,

TABLE 5.—*Percentage of Respondents Stressing Desirable and Undesirable Aspects of Drinking, by Various Factors*

	N	Desirable Aspect	Un-desirable Aspect	Chi Square
A. Occupational category I	15	60	40	
Occupational category VII	25	32	68	1.93
B. In unifying groups	90	61	39	
In partisan groups	105	36	64	11.08†
C. Worships regularly	142	41	59	
Worships occasionally	134	51	49	
Never worships	17	59	41	4.22
D. Catholics, Episcopalians and Lutherans	173	53	47	
Jews, Presbyterians, Reformed Churchmen, Methodists and Baptists	105	37	63	5.64*

*P<.05.   †P<.001.

Catholics, Episcopalians and Lutherans stressed the desirable aspect more commonly; while Jews, Presbyterians, Reformed Churchmen, Methodists and Baptists more commonly stressed the undesirable (Table 5-D).

AFFLUENCE AND INFLUENCE MAKE ABSTINENCE LESS LIKELY

Ten Relationships with Choice of Drinking or Abstinence

Cross-tabulations of the respondents' actual choice in regard to drinking or abstinence also show certain relationships. A greater proportion of third-generation Americans were drinkers than sixth- or later-generation (Table 6-A). There was a high incidence of

TABLE 6.—*Percentage of Drinkers and Abstainers, by Various Characteristics*

	N	Drinkers	Abstainers	Chi Square
A. 3d generation American	64	91	9	
6th or later generation American	33	55	45	14.84‡
B. From U.S.S.R., Baltics, Italy and Czechoslovakia	73	86	14	
From France, Scandinavia and Africa	60	47	53	22.29‡
C. Income constant	31	55	45	
Income greatly increased	37	89	11	8.54†
D. Job status not markedly improved	133	70	30	
Job status markedly improved	128	85	15	7.72†
E. Income below $6000	70	71	29	
Income $6000 to $10,000	154	73	27	
Income above $10,000	90	87	13	7.35*
F. Occupational category II	39	97	3	
Other occupational categories	234	81	19	5.22*
G. Class status 1, 2 & 3	141	85	15	
Class status 4 & 5	170	69	31	10.29†
H. High-school graduate	194	87	13	
Less than high school	127	60	40	29.97‡
I. Nonfundamentalist	243	81	19	
Fundamentalist	78	60	40	13.46‡
J. Worships regularly	155	70	30	
Worships occasionally or never	166	83	17	6.61*

*P<.05.   †P<.01.   ‡P<.001.

drinkers among ethnic groups of all backgrounds with only small differentials between them: the highest were among persons tracing their origins to the U.S.S.R., the Baltic countries (Lithuania, Estonia, Latvia), Italy and Czechoslovakia, the lowest among persons tracing theirs to the Scandinavian countries and to France, and among Negroes (Table 6-B).

There was a much higher percentage of drinkers among persons who had experienced a large increase in their level of income than among those whose income level had been relatively constant (Table 6-C). The same was true of those reporting a marked improvement in job status (Table 6-D). The higher the absolute level of present income the greater was the percentage of drinkers (Table 6-E). [In the national survey there was a constant increase in percentage of drinkers with increase in income (5, *p. 29*).] Abstainers were much less frequent in occupational category II of Hollingshead's occupational scale (i.e., business managers, proprietors of medium-sized businesses, and lesser professionals) than in any other category (Table 6-F). [In the national survey the largest proportions of drinkers were in the professional, semiprofessional, and technical, sales and managerial groups (5, *pp. 30-31*).] Abstinence was more common among the lower social classes as measured by Hollingshead's Index of Social Position (Table 6-G). [In the national survey there was a constant increase in percentage of drinkers with increase in social status (5, *pp. 24-28*).] Abstinence was also more common among those who had terminated their education early (Table 6-H). [In the national survey there was a constant increase in percentage of drinkers with increase in education (5, *pp. 31-32*).]

The incidence of abstainers increased with movement toward the more fundamentalist denominations in the religious spectrum—although in all denominations the abstainers were a minority (Table 6-I. [In the national survey the percentage of abstainers was much higher among those with marked religious fundamentalism (5, *pp. 154-164*).] There was a slightly lower percentage of drinkers among those who attended religious services regularly than among those who attended occasionally or never (Table 6-J). [In the national survey the proportion of abstainers was relatively high among those who attended church most frequently (5, *pp. 61-64*).]

One composite conclusion from all of this is that affluence and influence make abstinence less likely.

Intimate and Public Sociability
the Commonest Drinking Occasions

Those who drank were asked to identify the kinds of occasions on which they typically did so. Most commonly mentioned (by 56%) was before or at a regular meal; next most commonly (by 53%) was attendance at a public function—a party, dance or dinner. Quite a variety of situations was identified and, being defined by their cultural significance, they do not necessarily exclude one another as physical situations. Following are the drinking occasions and the percentage of the 245 drinkers reporting each:

Watching TV, reading, listening to music, 7%; parties, dances and dinners, 53%; cocktail parties, 19%; at a nightclub or cabaret, 19%; entertaining friends, relatives, neighbors as guests, 32%; visiting friends, relatives, neighbors, 35%; on weekends with friends, relatives, neighbors, 29%; with friends, relatives, neighbors (occasion unspecified), 16%; weddings, graduations, birthdays, "special occasions," 39%; before or at meals, 56%; picnics and the beach, 35%; on holidays, 12%; business meetings, luncheons, dinners, conventions, 11%; on a hot day, 3%; "out" with companions, 8%; during or after club meetings, 9%; after work, 11%; at home with the family, 24%; in connection with sports (hunting, ball games, bowling, etc.), 16%; after strenuous physical exertion, 2%; at a bar, 14%; before retiring, 2%; on vacation, 9%; for religious purposes, 2%; in cars, <1%; fraternity parties, <1%; at "wild" parties, 2%.

While some of these situations were mentioned by only a small percentage of the respondents, the following were mentioned by 30% or more: entertaining friends, relatives and neighbors; visiting friends, relatives and neighbors; attending special events like weddings, graduations and birthdays; participating in recreation on picnics or at the beach. It is clear from this that the drinking reported is overwhelmingly drinking in company and in the context of a meaningful occasion. Extremely few mentions were given to situations lacking social interaction, such as watching TV, reading, listening to music, on a hot day, after strenuous physical exertion, before retiring. Situations such as these, where it appeared that people drank because they needed alcohol and for no other reason, were acknowledged by fewer than 8%. Only 10% said they ever drank alone. All the drinking occasions a person mentioned were classified according to whether they were tied into more intimate or more impersonal relationships. For 87% of drinkers, one-half or more of their drinking occasions were connected with the more intimate kind of relationship.

It is also interesting that only 14% mentioned drinking at a public bar. The institution specializing in the serving of liquor can hardly be the symbolic focus of drinking in the modern American's mind. One is led to ask whether it has assumed some more specific significance for some more specific clientele. Who are the people who concentrate their drinking in public bars, who are the people who do some but not all of their drinking there, and why do they go there?

The respondents were asked to name all the different types of occasions on which they sometimes drank, in order to see whether there was variety in these. More than 75% acknowledged at least three different types of occasion. They were also asked to identify the two drinking situations that were most important to them. There was a great dispersion in the responses to that particular question, and they are given in Table 7. It can hardly be said that there was any set of situations standardized for the population as *the* occasions most appropriate for drinking. While the percentage nominating any one of them was certainly not large, the greatest number of mentions as the situation of first importance went to the following: at home with family (11%), and with meals at home (10%). (At home before meals was also mentioned by 8%). Mention of comparable frequency was given to entertaining friends, relatives and neighbors (9%); to attending parties, dinners and dances (8%); and to socializing with friends on weekends (8%). The most frequently mentioned drinking situations of second importance were the following: attending parties, dinners and dances (12%); socializing with friends on weekends (11%); visiting friends, relatives, neighbors (7%); attending weddings (6%). In the company of family, kinfolk and friends, and in the public observance of sociability, the practice of drinking thus finds its commonest uses.

THE TYPES OF DRINKING — FACILITATION THE MOST PREVALENT

The central question in the present study was to discover the significance of his drinking or abstinence to the person concerned—

TABLE 7.—*Drinking Situations Nominated as of First and Second Importance by the 245 Drinkers, in Per Cent*

	First	Second
Watching TV, reading, listening to music	1	3
With friends on weekends	8	11
Parties, dinners, and dances	8	12
Cocktail parties	4	4
At nightclub or cabaret	4	4
Entertaining friends, relatives, neighbors	9	6
Weddings	5	7
Other special occasions (excluding weddings)	1	2
Visiting friends, relatives, neighbors	5	7
Before meals (out)	2	3
Before meals (at home)	8	1
With meals (out)	<1	<1
With meals (at home)	10	3
Picnics and the beach	3	5
Holidays	2	2
Conventions	0	<1
At lunch (out)	0	1
Business affairs	1	1
On a hot day	0	1
Club meetings	2	2
After work	2	0
At home with the family	11	3
Bowling	2	2
Other sporting events (excluding bowling)	1	1
After strenuous physical exertion	1	0
At a tavern or bar	2	2
Before retiring	<1	0
With friends, relatives, neighbors (unspecified)	6	5
Religious ceremonial	1	<1
None	2	10

significance in terms of the typologies presented in Chapter 1. This was judged, by two independent raters, in reference to the drinking situations that the respondents claimed to be of first and second importance (Table 8).[1]

Whatever the situation named as being of first importance, the predominant meaning given to it was a combination of ornamental and facilitation drinking—49% drank that way. For another 24%

---

[1] The method of making these judgments is described in the Notes on the Indices deposited with NAPS. See footnote 3 of Chapter 4, p. 39.

TABLE 8.—*Types of Drinking Situations Nominated as of First and Second Importance by 245 Drinkers, in Per Cent*

	First	Second
Ornamental (O)	12	11
Facilitation (F)	24	21
Assuagement (A)	3	1
Retaliation	0	0
O + F + A	4	6
O + F	49	40
A + F	7	12
Not classifiable	2	9

the drinking was purely for facilitation, for another 12% it was purely ornamental. By addition of these and the other relevant combinations, ornamental drinking was found to be a component for 65% of drinkers and facilitation a component for 83%. In comparison, assuagement drinking was rare, and retaliation drinking was not found in the sample. Assuagement was the whole meaning in 3% and a component in another 11%. Similar percentages were found according to situations of second importance. The absence in the sample of any case of retaliation drinking is presumably an indication of its extreme rarity—at least in suburbia. This raises the question whether drinkers of this type are found mainly on Skid Row or, at least, among persons who are not represented in a household-type sample.

Direct statements on the meaning of their drinking confirm the impression that facilitation is the rationale for drinking most commonly entertained. Moreover, it is the facilitation of relaxation that is usually meant. Possibly the general prevalence of this relaxation idea is the most significant finding of the present study, and the full implications of it will be discussed later. When drinkers were given the opportunity to say in their own words what their drinking meant, some mentioned a single factor, some a combination of factors. There was no standard response forthcoming from any large percentage; but 16% said their drinking was relaxing and an aid to fraternization, 15% that it was relaxing purely and simply, 14% that it was relaxing and a form of recreation, 9% that it was relaxing, a form of recreation and an aid to fraternization besides. In combination with still other factors relaxation was mentioned by another 23%. If all these mentions are summed, 76% (or 63% according to situation of second importance) included mention of relaxation, and this is much the greatest frequency of mention given to any one factor.

It is revealing to extract from this general emphasis on the instrumental use of alcohol the specific evidence that a person's drinking is seldom central to his self-identification. A set of questions aimed to discover whether the practice of drinking made the person feel more complete in defined ways. Overwhelmingly, these questions were answered negatively, suggesting that the practice is not defined positively by most people, nor something with which they particularly identify. The great majority of men and women claimed they did not feel that the practice of drinking would make one more masculine or more feminine, more adult, more acceptable at work or at home, a more athletic type, a less hard-driving person, closer to people who may be very different from oneself, more a citizen, more a man or woman of the world, more a person of culture and taste, more a man or woman of religion, a more sophisticated person, or a person of greater dignity. There were, however, some positive answers to all questions in the set. The largest was 26% for the feeling that the practice of drinking made one closer to people who may be very different from oneself, followed by 18% for the feeling that it made one more adult.

The type of drink favored on occasions rated as important is presented in Table 9: in situations of first importance, 36% preferred beer, 27% a mixed drink, 23% a cocktail, 16% wine, 9% distilled spirits. [In the national survey, of wine, beer and spirits, wine was the least frequently drunk (5, *pp. 65-70*).] On any single occasion, two beers, highballs or cocktails were more commonly favored than only one.

THE INFREQUENT DRINKING OF MOST DRINKERS

The frequency with which persons made occasions for drinking varied tremendously. This is a characteristic of the drinking population that should be borne in mind just as much as their disposition to emphasize the favorable or unfavorable aspect of drinking. Table 10 gives the complete findings: 55% were unwilling to state any other frequency for the drinking occasion of most importance to them than "from time to time"; only 20% observed the occasion

TABLE 9.—*Favored Type of Drink in Drinking Situations Nominated as of First and Second Importance by 243 Drinkers, in Per Cent*

	First	Second
Rye	1	0
Cocktail	23	20
Whisky (unspecified)	4	4
Wine	16	9
Scotch	4	4
Punch	0	<1
Beer	36	37
Punch and cocktail	1	0
Mixed drink	27	33
Vodka	<1	<1
Rum	0	<1
Gin	1	1
Bourbon	<1	<1
Champagne	0	1
Brandy	0	<1
Unspecified (implying "whatever person enjoys")	8	11
Anything (implying "will drink anything which happens to be around")	1	<1
Not classifiable	3	4

more frequently than once a month; only 10% indicated it was a daily practice. [In the national survey 63% of drinkers were classified as infrequent or light drinkers (5, *pp. 18-24*).]

ORNAMENTAL, FACILITATION AND ASSUAGEMENT DRINKING ALL INSTITUTIONALIZED

A second question of importance in this study was whether the forms of drinking and abstinence actually practiced were institu-

TABLE 10.—*Frequency of Drinking Situations Nominated as of First and Second Importance by 243 Drinkers, in Per Cent*

	First	Second
Time to time	55	65
Once a year	1	<1
Several times a year	9	7
Once a month	5	5
2 or 3 times a month	3	7
Once a week	7	6
Several times a week	8	5
Once a day	10	2
Daily when on vacation	0	1
Not classifiable	2	3

INDIVIDUAL CHOICE AND SOCIAL SANCTION

tionalized, whether they were socially recognized and protected by sanction or simply idiosyncratic to the person. Seven indicators of that kind of embedding in society were selected:[2] (*i*) endorsement of the person's practice in some social systems around him of increasing inclusiveness, viz., the drinking group concerned, other groups in the community having any concern regarding it, and the whole of America; (*ii*) symbolization of the situation by its being defined clearly and in detail; (*iii*) existence of agencies charged with internalizing the practice; (*iv*) existence of external sanctions for reinforcing the practice; (*v*) anchorage of the practice in social role by being a part of what its fulfillment requires; (*vi*) existence of a public rationale for the practice; (*vii*) operation of mechanisms of control in response to deviance from normal observance of the practice.

Each person's first and second most important drinking situation was scored for each of these factors separately on a 4-point scale, and then scored for all of them in combination on a 4-point scale, assuming all factors to be of equal weight. The scores for any specific situation (e.g., at home with the family, with friends on weekends, at weddings) were then combined to see whether some of these were more highly institutionalized than others. Unfortunately, the numbers of cases in the subclasses were too small to make these comparisons meaningful. The data on institutionalization were therefore put to the following use: Disregarding the particular character of the drinking situation, I examined how extensively the over-all pattern of drinking practice is institutionalized, the image of that general pattern being, of course, the one just outlined.

Table 11 gives the percentage of drinkers with scores below and above the midpoint on each of the indicators separately and in combination, for each of two drinking situations. On the assumption that an item score above the midpoint shows that a practice is institutionalized in that aspect, and that an average score above it indicates that it is institutionalized in general, 75% (or 58% in situations of second importance) scored as institutionalized in general. Most of the drinking, thus, can be said to be institutionalized drinking.

---

[2] The method of abstracting this information from the questionnaire is described in the Notes on the Indices. See footnote 3 of Chapter 4, p. 39.

TABLE 11.—*Percentage of 243 Drinkers Above and Below Midpoint on Each of Seven Indicators of Institutionalization of Drinking Situations of First and Second Importance*

	FIRST			SECOND		
	Above	Below	NC*	Above	Below	NC*
System-endorsement	52	43	5	51	35	14
Degree of symbolization	63	32	5	57	29	14
Internalization	49	46	5	52	33	15
External sanctions	45	50	5	40	45	14
Role anchorage	54	41	5	34	51	14
Public rationale	45	50	5	40	46	14
Social control	33	63	5	29	56	14
Institutionalization (i.e., average of above items)	75	20	5	58	27	14

* NC=not classifiable.

In the case of the separate items, scores were typically divided in roughly equal numbers around the midpoint, with more than half of the cases coming above midpoint on four of the items, more than half of them below it on three. It is interesting to notice on which items there were more unequal divisions. Symbolization showed the greatest preponderance of higher scores over lower, followed by role-anchorage in the case of the first drinking situation and system-wide endorsement in the case of the second. A possible interpretation of this is that what comes first in anyone's practice of drinking is a knowledge of what to do and how to build it into one's public deportment and social acceptability. The greatest preponderance of lower scores over higher was on social control of deviance, followed, in the case of the first situation, by a public rationale for practice. A possible interpretation of this is that what comes late is any awareness of a public meaning attributed to drinking and, last of all, any preparedness to cope with the misuse of alcohol.

Cross-tabulation did allow exploration of one important question regarding institutionalization: whether ornamental drinking was more highly institutionalized than the other types. Table 12 gives collapsed cross-tabulations, for the person's two important drinking situations, of the type of drinking and the institutionalization score. The uncollapsed tables showed that all the identified forms of drinking are more frequently institutionalized than not. The dif-

TABLE 12.—*Relationships between Type of Drinking[a] and Institutionalization Score*

	O Only	O + F + A or O + F
A. Low institutionalization score (first situation)	10	16
High institutionalization score (first situation)	17	111[b]
B. Low institutionalization score (second situation)	7	30
High institutionalization score (second situation)	17	78

[a] O=ornamental; F=facilitation; A=assuagement.
[b] Chi square=18.05; $P<.01$.

ferences between them are not considerable, but it is interesting to observe, in the case of the first situation, that purely ornamental drinking has the lowest percentage and that facilitation is higher, while facilitation in combination with ornamental drinking is higher still. The highest percentage of all attaches to the combination of ornamental, facilitation and assuagement drinking, although, of course, the number of cases in this class is quite small. It is clear from this that facilitation drinking is sanctioned as much as ornamental, and it seems rather likely that assuagement drinking is sanctioned too. Not only do people choose to drink for these reasons, it seems they are encouraged to think this sort of drinking appropriate.

THE TYPES OF ABSTINENCE—OBJECTION TO FACILITATION DRINKING

Just as the study tried to discriminate between the different meanings given to drinking by the drinkers, it sought to discriminate between different reasons underlying abstinence. For, no more than drinking is abstinence a single thing. A significant finding is that 26% of the 76 abstainers practiced "indifference" abstinence, while 22% practiced "moral" abstinence, 3% "religious" abstinence, and 3% "respectability" abstinence. But each of these also occurred in combinations: religious + respectability, 1%; moral + religious, 17%; indifference + moral, 12%; moral + religious + respectability, 13%; moral + respectability, 3%. Hence, whether alone or in combination, moral abstinence was found in 67%, religious in 34%, respectability in 20%.

The existence of this range of different concerns amply justifies the attempt to be discriminating. It also shows that much the most common source of objection to drinking was to its facilitation use. This is particularly interesting in view of the fact that it was in terms of its facilitation use that drinkers most commonly justified their drinking. Apparently these abstainers refrained from drinking for fear they would come to lean on alcohol as a crutch, making it do things for them that they thought they should learn to do for themselves. That this mirror-imaging occurs between the main justifications for drinking and abstinence is probably only to be expected. It is the issue as defined that people will divide over when they take sides. So it may be with respect to drinking as having this possibility that people will make their choice.

ABSTINENCE INSTITUTIONALIZED AS AN INDIVIDUAL OPTION

Once again as with drinking, an attempt was made to find whether abstinence was institutionalized. Being by its nature a negative thing, an avoidance and an exception, indicators for this had to be selected with some circumspection. The following were used: (i) endorsement from outside of the right of the individual to choose for himself, on the condition that he concede the same option to others; (ii) symbolization of the grounds for individualistic abstinence in terms like this: "it [drinking] is just not right for me but it could be all right for another person"; (iii) ability to name typical occasions where he had been allowed to decline a drink; (iv) ability to give a purely private rationale in detailed objections. Each respondent was scored for each of these factors separately on a 4-point scale, and then scored on a 4-point scale for all of them in combination, all factors being treated as of equal weight.

Table 13 gives the percentage of abstainers with scores below

TABLE 13.—*Percentage of 76 Abstainers Above and Below Midpoint on Each of Four Indicators of Institutionalization*

	Above	Below
Endorsement of right of private option	62	38
Degree of symbolization	84	15
Nomination of situations of refusal	65	36
Private rationale of objection	65	36
Institutionalization		
(i.e., average of above items)	59	41

and above the midpoint on each of the indicators separately and in combination; 59% scored as institutionalized in general. This indicates, then, that the practice of abstinence as an individual option is also institutionalized. But it is of some importance that it is viewed in that particular light. It is viewed negatively, as a right to opt out of the standard practice, for individual reasons. Those reasons are not expected to have any general validity, nor is there supposed to be any single, consolidated rationale for abstinence in the society as a whole. And, as we have just seen, those who chose to exercise this option did so for at least four reasons.

LEARNING TO DRINK OR ABSTAIN—
SPECIAL IMPORTANCE OF THE FAMILY

Supplementary light on institutionalization comes from additional details on the induction into drinking of a new generation: 73% reported that their parents were more important than anyone else in helping them to make a choice regarding alcohol; 56% were openly appreciative of the influence their parents had exercised, and only 5% harbored resentment about parents' influence. In 60% of the respondents the parents had sought to exercise influence by example only, in 8% by introducing the person to drinking situations, in 25% by trying to dissuade the person from drinking by argument. Most people felt that the stance they eventually took had been voluntarily embraced: 60% said their stance was individually worked out, 27% that they had copied that of someone known to them, 9% that it was a considered modification of the practice of someone known to them.

Perhaps note should be taken at this point of the general family conformity that obtained in regard to drinking practice. It was much more common to find that husband and wife were both drinkers (73%) or abstainers (13%) than that they diverged from one another on this choice. Where they did, it was commoner for the husband to be the drinker and the wife the abstainer (11%) than the other way about (2%). The situation between the generations was similar. In 75% of families, all children aged 21 and over conformed with the parent of the same sex in being a drinker or abstainer. [In the national survey moderate or heavy drinkers were more likely than others to say that their parents drank twice a month or more (5, *pp. 77-80*).] The numbers here were not large enough, however, to show whether there was any greater tendency, when divergence did occur, for drinking parents to have abstaining children or vice versa.

The age at which the person remembers having his first drink and the age at which he eventually adopted drinking as a practice are given in Table 14. Half the respondents had sampled alcohol

TABLE 14.—*Age at First Drink (N=250) and Age at Which Respondent Started to Drink Habitually (N=245), in Per Cent*

Age	First Drink	Age	Habit Drink
<11	13	<18	8
11-15	18	18-20	27
16-20	49	21-25	34
21-25	12	26-30	6
26+	2	31-40	6
Unclassified	7	40+	2
		Unclassified	18

by the age of 20—hardly a significant finding. More significant is the fact that 34% had made a practice of drinking by the age of 20 and another 34% had done so between ages 21 and 25. [In the national survey 53% adopted the practice before age 21, 79% before age 25 (5, *pp. 101-103*).] Hence it is clear that, in the typical case, the learning of drinking was part of full socialization into adult status. Cross-tabulations revealed one weak association with age: Adopting drinking as a practice before age 18 was more characteristic of persons with less education: of the 20 drinkers with less than 7 years of education, 4 started drinking before age 18, compared with 16 of the 225 drinkers with more education.

Chapter 6

Ideals to Guide

PEOPLE have ideals by which they can judge their own conduct, and standards by reference to which they seek to make their choices. We gain depth in our understanding of behavior if we can view it against these orienting tendencies. This is especially true of behavior in areas like the one under study, where there is ambiguity and where alternative choices can seem justifiable to different persons. An attempt was therefore made to penetrate to this level.

GENERAL AGREEMENT ON THE IDEAL OF DRINKING APPROVED— EXCEPT REGARDING FACILITATION

A projective test was developed to detect what ideal of drinking was approved and to see whether the type of drinking actually practiced was in line with this ideal.[1] Table 15 gives the distribu-

TABLE 15.—*Percentage of Respondents (N=321) Expressing Opinions of Drinking and Abstinence Types*

Drinking	For	Neutral	Against
Ornamental	83	12	5
Facilitation	24	26	50
Assuagement	2	12	86
Retaliation	0	10	90
Abstinence			
Indifference	87	8	5
Moral	64	13	23
Religious	73	12	16
Respectability	42	22	36
Outward drinking only	48	21	31
Avoidance of occasion	28	26	46

[1] The projective test is Part III of the Interview Schedule. The sets of items testing for each type are described in the Notes on the Indices. Both items have been deposited with NAPS; see footnote 3 of Chapter 4, p. 39.

tion of responses; and it should be remembered, of course, that these are the aggregated responses of drinkers and abstainers both. It is interesting to observe, once again, that the one big division is over facilitation. Whereas people were overwhelmingly in favor of ornamental drinking and against assuagement and retaliation drinking, only 50% were against facilitation, 24% were in favor of it and another 26% were neutral. Furthermore, this small number of approvals must be contrasted with the fact that 83% of drinkers acknowledged using their drinking for facilitation. Cross-tabulation showed that only 31% of those in whose own drinking facilitation was a component actually approved of it. It is apparent, then, that some who practiced this style of drinking did so with a bad conscience, since they were violating their own standards. In any case, it is clear that public opinion on this particular use of drinking is not unequivocal in the same way that it is in regard to the other three uses.

It was interesting to discover what amount of agreement existed among members of the same families in their approval of the different uses of alcohol. Spouse, mother-child and father-child relationships were the ones examined. For all uses and for all relationships, agreement was more common than divergence, while the latter was always split in direction, there being some more in favor and others less in favor of any particular practice. Agreement on the retaliation use was more marked than agreement on the other uses. The most marked cases of divergence were 32% of children favoring facilitation more than their mothers, 30% disparaging assuagement more than their mothers, and 29% favoring ornamental drinking more than their fathers.

THE APPROVED IDEAL OF ABSTINENCE

Projection scores on the different types of abstinence were also given to everyone interviewed. These are also shown in Table 15. To indifference abstinence 87% gave approval, to religious abstinence 73%, to moral abstinence 64%, to respectability abstinence only 42%. Two stances on drinking were also portrayed that were additional to those considered at the level of practice. One was drinking without identification with the practice (the person is really an abstainer at heart but will drink "when he absolutely can't get out of it" in order not to offend): 48% approved of this stance, 21% were neutral, and 31% disapproved. The other was the practice of avoiding the occasions of drinking simply because the person wants to avoid drinking. For this there was no comparable degree of support: only 28% approved.

As with drinking, it was interesting to discover the amount of agreement existing among members of the same families in their attitudes to the varieties of abstinence. Here again, the striking thing is the high agreement in attitude within the family. The only important divergences were 50% showing more approval than their fathers for respectability abstinence, 43% more approval than their fathers for the avoidance of drinking occasions in order to avoid drinking, and 34% more approval than their mothers for the same thing.

SECULARIZATION: THE CAPACITY FOR RATIONAL DISCRIMINATION

An important adaptive trait in the modern world is a capacity to make discriminating judgments on possible courses of action. In a world so subject to change one needs to know where to hold on and where to let go. Simply to be massively conservative or radical in one's reactions can be equally maladaptive. Hence knowing whether a person is conservative or radical is often not so relevant as knowing whether he is discriminating enough to accept changes which are adaptive and reject those which are not. Can he avoid throwing out the baby with the bath water at the same time as he avoids being a blind reactionary?

A general measure was developed of the individual's readiness to do that kind of thing; of his readiness, that is, to accept only those changes which to the discriminating judgment would seem adaptive. The set of items in Part IV of the interview schedule was designed to test for this. On each item the respondent endorses one out of three statements: one of these indicates rational discrimination, one low discrimination in the direction of reaction, one low discrimination in the opposite direction, a direction that might perhaps be called laxity. The aggregate measure was called

an "index of secularization."[2] For, however various and confusing
the uses of that term may have been, "secularization" is essentially
this capacity to endorse changes which appeal to reason through
being adaptive.[3]

Half of the respondents indicated a readiness to endorse rational
adaptations, 12% earned a score which showed low discrimination
in the direction of laxity and 38% a score showing low discrimination in the direction of reaction. Conformity within the family in
respect to secularization was also explored. Here again, there was
more intrafamily conformity than lack of it. Where the children
did diverge from the parental generation in being less discriminating, divergence from the parents in the direction of laxity was two
to three times as frequent as in the direction of reaction.

Relationships with Secularization

Cross-tabulations showed relationships which further illuminate
the nature of secularization. With decreasing education there was
a decreasing percentage of center scores and an increasing percentage of reaction scores (Table 16-A). It was much more char-

TABLE 16.—*Percentage of Respondents with Center, Laxity and
Reaction Scores on the Secularization Index, by Various Characteristics*

	N	Center	Laxity	Reaction	Chi Square
A. *Education*					
College graduate	86	65	8	27	
High-school graduate	108	55	6	39	
Less than high school	126	37	19	44	22.27‡
B. *Social Class*					
I	29	62	10	28	
V	55	27	20	53	9.60†
C. *Income*					
Down	33	36	24	40	
Same or up	287	52	10	38	6.43*
D. *Religion*					
Catholics and Jews	177	45	14	41	
Protestants	143	57	10	33	4.25
E. *Drinker*	245	56	10	34	
Abstainer	75	31	17	52	15.09‡

*$P<.05$.   †$P<.01$.   ‡$P<.001$.

[2] Described in the Notes on the Indices. See footnote 3 of Chapter 4, p. 39.
[3] My discussion of the definition of this term has been given elsewhere (9,
pp. 349-364).

acteristic of high-status than low-status persons to have center scores; and it was more characteristic of the latter to have reaction scores (Table 16-B). A smaller percentage of those with a history of reduction in income had center scores than of those whose income had increased or stayed the same (Table 16-C). No important difference in secularization was associated with different degrees of religious observance or nonobservance. While the difference was not significant, a higher percentage of Protestants had center scores than did Catholics or Jews (Table 16-D).

There was no relationship between secularization and the respondent's memberships being in organizations with a local or cosmopolitan orientation. But the relationship with drinking was the question of chief concern, of course. Here it was found to be more characteristic of drinkers than abstainers to have center scores, more characteristic of abstainers than of drinkers to have reaction scores (Table 16-E). This suggests that the choice between drinking and abstaining is one that does demand discrimination, and that the person practiced in discrimination is better prepared to embrace the ambiguities in the former alternative.

IGNORANCE OVER IMPAIRMENT AND PROBLEM DRINKING

Two foci of ambiguity confronting the person who chooses to drink are the possibility of impairment while driving and the possibility of anyone's drinking becoming "problem drinking." It seems that most of the drinkers were somewhat at a loss in regard to both these matters.

Of the drinkers, 42% acknowledged having leisure activities that involved both drinking and driving, 62% having leisure activities away from home that involved drinking, 97% some occasions for drinking away from home. This indicates that the necessity of making a journey following drinking has become quite widespread. Yet, what to do about it is not particularly clear to many. Most drinkers who drove were conscious of a need to make some change in the usual pattern of drinking before driving (83%). But most of them (52%) could not detail it in any other way than reducing the amount of liquor consumed, although they could not specify by how much; 16% considered it necessary to abstain completely. The remainder had no rule to go by.

A set of questions was asked concerning problem drinking and alcoholism: 63% acknowledged they had a responsibility toward a person who drank with them if it became apparent that that person was headed for problem drinking. Another 17% saw the responsibility as not theirs but wholly or mainly that of the person's family; 2% as not theirs but that of a clergyman; 2% as not theirs but that of the person's physician.

There was no single sign or set of signs by which most respondents would recognize that a person was headed for problem drinking: 15% said they would expect to see evidences of some kind of compulsion to drink; 14% reported they could "tell by the person's actions," but did not specify what the actions would be; 7% saw the evidence in the person always getting drunk; 6% in his "consuming one drink after another" on any occasion when he drank at all.

For a person who drank with them who already was taken to be "a clear alcoholic," only 51% recognized that they themselves had some responsibility. Another 24% saw the responsibility as not theirs but wholly or mainly that of the person's family; 3% as not theirs but that of the person's physician; 3% as not theirs but that of a clergyman. In this matter too there was no single sign or set of signs by which most persons would recognize the condition in question. Indeed 24% frankly acknowledged that they would not have any way of knowing when a person was an alcoholic; 13% reported it was when a person was unable to be without alcoholic beverages; 10% when he "consumed one drink after another" on any occasion when he drank at all; 8% when he was intoxicated most of the time; 8% when his behavior exhibited a general loss of responsibility.

The findings reported in this chapter betray a fairly pervasive lack of assurance over guiding principles, although within families a position once adopted commonly becomes shared. There is a division of opinion over the legitimacy of facilitation drinking, and many of those who say they disapprove of it practice it. There is uncertainty over drinking before driving and over the way to handle problem drinking and alcoholism. There is, finally, a considerable range in the capacity for rational, discriminating judgment in general and it is more common for this to be exhibited by drinkers than by abstainers.

Chapter 7

The Right Deed for
the Wrong Reason

IN THE THIRD CHAPTER the crucial question was raised: What sense of meaningfulness in drinking has been recovered by modern Americans in view of their history? An answer to this question can now be proposed.

It is clear that the one benign or functional kind of drinking, which I call ornamental, is not the one that dominates in people's minds. Only about a tenth of drinkers drank in an exclusively ornamental way. And, while ornamental drinking was very generally approved in principle, a large proportion of people did not give approval to that exclusively. In addition, abstinence is not seen as it would be seen if ornamental drinking were the norm. Rather than being as accepted and expected as is drinking, a live alternative, it is considered to be part of the right of the individual to be a nonconformist for idiosyncratic reasons.

From among the assortment of reasons for which drinking is engaged in, it is facilitation that emerges as predominant. One is glad to have it on tap to help one relax. The assumption is that daily life generates considerable tension, and alcohol is the standard means of finding relief. A special aspect of this is help in relaxing in the presence of people with whom one senses some barrier and inhibition. Rather than the company of people being itself relaxing, as occurs when the feeling of community allows one to "lose oneself," it appears that people can typically be in situations where company is distinctly prickly. One is thus almost astonished to see Horton's (19) primitive drinking situation repeated in the suburban drawing-room. The modern equivalent of the primitive's anxiety-inducing culture contact is the cultural pluralism of neighbors and work associates who cannot count on beliefs and values being shared. In Chapter 2 I took note of the diverse and cross-cutting community allegiances that exist in one locality. Such in-group solidarities present barriers of social distance to the out-groups, and the suburbanite walks into them continually.

Having learned to appreciate alcohol for its assistance in sur-mounting these barriers, people justify its use in these terms as much as in ornamental terms. Hence there is a blunting of discrim-ination and this, apparently, becomes progressive. From finding alcohol useful in the attempt to bridge social distance one can find it useful to relieve anxiety at the points of contact where, it even-tually comes to appear, no bridging can ever be expected. In this way its use for assuagement is justified. So it comes about that all three kinds of drinking—ornamental, facilitation and assuage-ment—are institutionalized and the young grow up in a culture where no discriminations between them are drawn to their atten-tion. The doorway into problem drinking and alcoholism therefore always stands wide open. These things have their roots in practices that are normally sanctioned. It is probably not surprising, then, that few people understand when and by what signs drinking turns into problem drinking. For it is simply an outgrowth of the de-pendence on alcohol's assistance that is commonly endorsed. One would think that if these developments are to be eradicated, the surgery would have to be applied sooner.

Not that some people do not already know better than they do, and better than they encourage others to do. When a mirror is held up to assuagement drinking as an ideal, it is rejected by almost everyone. When facilitation drinking is similarly reflected, fewer than a quarter of the people give positive endorsement to it. Here a decided ambivalence is apparent. Yet it is a kind of ambivalence that can be found in other areas of life—a discrepancy between what people aspire to and what they will tolerate because of com-promising practicalities. Other kinds of ambivalence about alcohol have been described by other authors. Ullman (34) recognized that a personal ambivalence could be induced by inconsistent standards, and thought it could produce alcoholism. Simmons (32) observed a more realistic kind of ambivalence in the Lunahuaneños. It arose out of the fact that the effects of alcohol could be either pleasant or degrading.

But the ambivalence I am reporting betokens something else. It is like the memory of a more ideal state or a longing for attainment to it. It is as though people were half-conscious of the fact that a more ideal form of drinking could come, yet only with a more ideal society—one where community prevailed. The failures of civilization implicit in the institutionalization of facilitation and assuagement drinking are a failure, fundamentally, of community.

There is a typically timid approach to social problems which goes directly to the most superficial and short-range solution. Applied to the present problem, it would probably recommend that people should learn simply to relax without artificial, chemical aids. There would, of course, be much gain if this could be done. If people could learn to work, yogalike, in a more relaxed way, they would not need periodically to be artificially let down. If, in addition, they made provision to punctuate their lives with constructive recreation, they would be routinely refreshed in a more satisfying way. A second and less superficial recommendation might draw attention to the need to moderate competitive ambition and thereby preserve self-acceptance. People who accept themselves are not wanting always to impress and are therefore better able to meet others without alcoholic anesthesia. Yet these, as well as a variety of other remedies that might be proposed, are piecemeal, and they invoke a chain of other required conditions that really culminate in the need for community.

Kenneth Clark (7) tells of the profound sense of community that motivated the men and women who built the civilization epitomized in the cathedral at Chartres.

"In the year 1144, they say, when the towers [of Chartres] seemed to be rising as if by magic, the faithful harnessed themselves to the carts which were bringing stone, and dragged them from the quarry to the cathedral. The enthusiasm spread throughout France. Men and women came from far away carrying heavy burdens of provisions for the workmen—wine, oil, corn. Amongst them were lords and ladies, pulling carts with the rest. There was perfect discipline, and a most profound silence. All hearts were united and each man forgave his enemies" (7, p. 56).

The clock cannot be turned back and one would not expect that particular community to materialize again. But that same quality of community could come again.

I would venture the opinion that drinking practice is a sensitive barometer of community strength. It will scarcely come exactly into place until men from a score of traditions commit themselves together to common beliefs and values. I would also venture the opinion that the values that will win the necessary allegiance will be spiritual values. It is these that have perennial appeal because of the lasting satisfaction they give. It is these that lift men out of themselves by absorbing them into a more inclusive scheme of things. To be thus carried out of the utilitarian world and its egoistic anxiety is something everyone seems to crave. The widespread use of other drugs that has been added to alcohol use in our time can be viewed as a kind of agonized reassertion that man was not made for a purely utilitarian life. Yet drugs make a pathetically artificial entry to the other world where he is more at home. To come through in a real way to that other world he must have the support of fellow-seekers.

Bibliography

1. BACON, S. D. Alcohol and complex society. Pp. 78-93. In: PITTMAN, D. J. and SNYDER, C. R., eds. Society, culture, and drinking patterns. New York; Wiley; 1962.

2. BALES, R. F. Attitudes toward drinking in the Irish culture. Pp. 157-187. In: PITTMAN, D. J. and SNYDER, C. R., eds. Society, culture, and drinking patterns. New York; Wiley; 1962.

3. BISMUTH, H. and MENAGE, C. Aspects de l'alcoolisme dans les états de langue française de l'Afrique Occidentale; rapport général. Paris; Haut Comité d'Etude et d'Information sur l'Alcoolisme; 1960.

4. BUNZEL, R. The role of alcoholism in two central American cultures. Psychiatry 3: 361-387, 1940.

5. CAHALAN, D., CISIN, I. H. and CROSSLEY, H. M. American drinking practices; a national study of drinking behavior and attitudes. (Rutgers Center of Alcohol Studies, Monogr. No. 6.) New Brunswick, NJ; 1969.

6. CARSON, G. The social history of bourbon; an unhurried account of our star-spangled American drink. New York; Dodd, Mead; 1963.

7. CLARK, K. Civilisation, a personal view. London; British Broadcasting Corporation & John Murray; 1969.

8. DURKHEIM, E. The division of labour in society. (SIMPSON, G., transl.) New York; Macmillan; 1933.

9. FALLDING, H. Secularization and the sacred and profane. Sociol. Quart. 8: 349-364, 1967.

10. FALLDING, H. The sociological task. Englewood Cliffs, NJ; Prentice-Hall; 1968.

11. FIELD, P. B. A new cross-cultural study of drunkenness. Pp. 48-74. In: PITTMAN, D. J. and SNYDER, C. R., eds. Society, culture, and drinking patterns. New York; Wiley; 1962.

12. GUSFIELD, J. R. Symbolic crusade; status politics and the American temperance movement. Urbana; University of Illinois Press; 1963.

13. HANDLIN, O. The uprooted; the epic story of the great migrations that made the American people. Boston; Little, Brown; 1952.

14. HANDLIN, O. The American people in the twentieth century. Cambridge, MA; Harvard University Press; 1954.

15. HEATH, D. B. Drinking patterns of the Bolivian Camba. Pp. 22-36. In: PITTMAN, D. J. and SNYDER, C. R., eds. Society, culture, and drinking patterns. New York; Wiley; 1962.

16. HERBERG, W. Protestant—Catholic—Jew; an essay in American religious sociology. New York; Doubleday; 1960.

17. HOLLINGSHEAD, A. B. Two factor index of social position. New Haven, CT; 1957.

18. HOOVER, E. M. and VERNON, R. Anatomy of a metropolis. Cambridge, MA; Harvard University Press; 1959.

19. HORTON, D. The functions of alcohol in primitive societies; a cross-cultural study. Quart. J. Stud. Alc. 4: 199-320, 1943.

20. JELLINEK, E. M. The disease concept of alcoholism. Highland Park, NJ; Hillhouse Press; 1960.

21. LOLLI, G., SERIANNI, E., BANISSONI, F., GOLDER, G., MARIANI, A., Mc-CARTHY, R. G. and TONER, N. The use of wine and other alcoholic beverages by a group of Italians and Americans of Italian extraction. Quart. J. Stud. Alc. 13: 27-48, 1952.

22. McCARTHY, R. G. and DOUGLASS, E. M. Alcohol and social responsibility; a new educational approach. New York; Crowell; 1949.

23. McKINLAY, A. P. Roman sobriety in the later Republic. Classical Bull. 25: 27-28, 1949.

24. MELLICK, A. D. The story of an old farm; or life in New Jersey in the eighteenth century. Somerville, NJ; The Unionist-Gazette; 1889.

25. MENNINGER, K. A. Man against himself. New York; Harcourt, Brace; 1938.

26. MESSLER, A. Forty years at Raritan: eight memorial sermons with notes for a history of the Reformed Dutch churches in Somerset County, N.J. New York; A. Lloyd; 1873.

27. MOUCHOT, G. Letter from France. Int. J. Alc. Alcsm 1: 75-84, 1955.

28. PALOLA, E. G., DORPAT, T. L. and LARSON, W. R. Alcoholism and suicidal behavior. Pp. 511-534. In: PITTMAN, D. J. and SNYDER, C. R., eds. Society, culture, and drinking patterns. New York; Wiley; 1962.

29. RUBINGTON, E. 'Failure' as a heavy drinker; the case of the chronic-drunkenness offender on Skid Row. Pp. 146-156. In: PITTMAN, D. J. and SNYDER, C. R., eds. Society, culture, and drinking patterns. New York; Wiley; 1962.

30. SANGREE, W. H. The social functions of beer drinking in Bantu Tiriki. Pp. 6-21. In: PITTMAN, D. J. and SNYDER, C. R., eds. Society, culture, and drinking patterns. New York; Wiley; 1962.

31. SHIBUTANI, T. Society and personality, an interactionist approach to social psychology. Englewood Cliffs, NJ; Prentice-Hall; 1961.

32. SIMMONS, O. G. Ambivalence and the learning of drinking behavior in a Peruvian community. Amer. Anthrop. 62: 1018-1027, 1960.

33. SNYDER, C. R. Alcohol and the Jews; a cultural study of drinking and sobriety. (Rutgers Center of Alcohol Studies, Monogr. No. 1.) New Brunswick, NJ; 1958.

34. ULLMAN, A. D. Sociocultural backgrounds of alcoholism. Ann. Amer. Acad. polit. social Sci. 351: 48-54, 1958.

35. VERNON, R. Metropolis 1985; an interpretation of the findings of the New York metropolitan region study. Cambridge, MA; Harvard University Press; 1960.

36. VOORHEES, R. The Raritan and its early Holland settlers. Our Home: A Monthly Magazine 1: 496-498, 1873.

37. WASHBURNE, C. Primitive drinking; a study of the uses and functions of alcohol in preliterate societies. New Haven; College & University Press; 1961.

38. WEBER, M. The theory of social and economic organization. (HENDERSON,

A. M. and Parsons, T., transl.) New York; Oxford University Press; 1947.

39. Williams, P. H. and Straus, R. Drinking patterns of Italians in New Haven; utilization of the personal diary as a research technique. Quart. J. Stud. Alc. 11: 51-91, 250-308, 452-483, 586-629, 1950.

40. Winkler, A. Lyman Beecher and the temperance crusade. Quart. J. Stud. Alc. 33: 939-957, 1972.

Index of Names

Index of Subjects

71

Date Due
